"Fight for your dream and make your life an adventure."

- Gabriela & Ruben Gonzalez

Dream, Struggle, Victory

How to Think Like an Olympian to Realize Your Dreams

**By Gabriela Gonzalez
and Ruben Gonzalez**

Foreword by Olympic Gold Medalist Scott Hamilton

Olympia Press

Dream, Struggle, Victory

By Gabriela Gonzalez and Ruben Gonzalez

ISBN-10: 0975554751
ISBN-13: 978-0-9755547-5-3

Layout by Julie Smith
Cover Photograph by Dave Smith

Olympia Press
832-689-8282

What Others are Saying about "Dream, Struggle, Victory"

"I tell people every day that you've got to sacrifice to win. If you want to win big, you've got to do things you've probably never done before. *Dream, Struggle, Victory* is packed with stories of people who've done just that. This is a must-read for anyone who needs a quick shot of inspiration."

Dave Ramsey
**New York Times best-selling author
and nationally syndicated radio show host.**

"The compelling stories in *Dream, Struggle, Victory* will inspire you to set and reach Olympic-sized goals."

Tom Hopkins
**Author of the million-plus-selling book,
*How to Master the Art of Selling***

"Do you dream, struggle, want to win? Then you need to read, *Dream, Struggle, Victory.*"

Jeffrey J. Fox
Best selling author of *How to Be a Fierce Competitor.*

"When you discover a book by someone like Olympian Ruben Gonzalez who has been there and done it, take their advice and apply their knowledge to your own life. Read Ruben's book: *Dream, Struggle, Victory.*

Don Green
Executive Director of the Napoleon Hill Foundation

"Ruben achieved what few people do - realized his lifelong dream, now he teaches you how to do the same. The stories of determination, commitment and perseverance in *Dream, Struggle, Victory* will show you how to win in life. Buy it, read it, and apply it's timeless lessons."

Jack Canfield
Author of *The Success Principles*

"*Dream, Struggle, Victory* is a passionate call to action, challenging you to be the best that you can be."

Pat Williams
Orlando Magic Senior Vice President.
Author of *Leadership Excellence*

"This book will motivate you, stimulate you, stiffen your spine, and give you the drive to succeed in anything you do."

Brian Tracy
Author of *Million Dollar Habits*

"This book is will challenge you to be the best that you can be."

George Chavel
President and CEO, Sodexo

"The advice in *Dream, Struggle, Victory* is as relevant to a salesperson's quest to exceed quota as it is to a high school student working for an A in Chemistry. Whether your goal is small or large, personal or professional, short-term or long-term, the insights in this book will help you turn dreams into reality."

Marshall Goldsmith
Author of the New York Times bestsellers, *MOJO* and *What Got You Here Won't Get You There*.
Recognized as the Thinkers 50 most-influential leadership thinker in the world.

Table of Contents

Part 1 - Believe In Your Dream

Part 2 - Plan Ahead

Part 3 - Commit to Your Dream

Part 4 - Take Action

Part 5 - Don't Quit

Foreword by Olympic Gold Medalist Scott Hamilton

I meet a lot of people. That's my favorite consequence of becoming an Olympic athlete and having been able to pursue a professional skating career.

When I meet someone new, more times than not, I am asked one of two questions. The first is, "How many hours a day did you have to skate to become an Olympian?" The second is, "What do you think it takes to make it to the Olympics?"

These are great questions, and they are also the same ones that drive many athletes to do whatever it takes to achieve their dream. To become an Olympic athlete. "How many hours a day will it take?" "What do I have to do to get there?"

Every Olympic Dream story is basically the same. Or is it? That's what makes this book so intriguing.

Gabriela Gonzalez became fascinated with the Olympics while watching her father compete in the Men's Luge race at the 2010 Vancouver Winter Olympic Games. It was that event that inspired her to write a book that would help people better understand what it takes to reach their goals and dreams. And in the process of reading it's pages, possibly learn to think and behave more like Olympians.

I think that's pretty heady stuff for a girl who was then, just nine years old.

She researched her book by interviewing over 80 Olympic athletes from around the world asking them three simple questions. "How did you get your Olympic dream? What was the biggest struggle you had to face? and, What did it feel like when you realized your dream?"

All three are great questions. These are the athlete testimonials that were collected. They are meant to inspire everyone who reads them. Maybe to become more like an Olympian, or at least to be more equipped to handle life's struggles.

Gabriela purposely interviewed both Olympic medal and non-medal winners from around the world. She spoke with both Summer and Winter Olympians. Some are household names like Laura Wilkinson (diving), Shannon Miller (gymnastics), Greg Louganis (diving), Phil Mahre (alpine skiing), Jim Craig (ice hockey 1980 Miracle Team), Peter Vidmar (gymnastics), and Janet Evans (swimming). Others are participants that few have heard of, such as a cross country skier from Greenland and a pole vaulter from St. Lucia. Gabriela even spoke to me!

I see and meet many people that are frustrated. Life isn't giving them what they expect or what they feel they deserve. Life is hard on all of us, and sometimes we need a bit of a pep talk.

And in some really tough cases life can be hard because it hasn't been handed to them. There is a feeling of entitlement in this generation and many of those who feel entitled haven't quite figured out that they need to participate in life to make it better. What better way to awaken a champion spirit than to be inspired by stories of great struggle and sacrifice. The athletes in this book did it. And so can anyone that applies the principles shared in each of these stories.

This book will encourage you to do whatever it takes to accomplish great things. After reading *Dream, Struggle, Victory*, you will think, "If these principles worked for all these Olympic athletes, they will definitely work for me." The Olympians in this collection of short stories will serve as role models and mentors to you, showing you how to develop a winning attitude and also how to develop the character of a champion.

Dream, Struggle, Victory is not so much a book about sports, but more a book about life. It's a beautiful compilation of winning experiences that will touch your heart. It's filled with inspiring insights about believing in yourself and taking action to achieve your dreams regardless of the obstacles.

No matter how old you are, *Dream, Struggle, Victory* will help you develop the winning attitude that will help you achieve success in whatever you may choose to pursue, whether it be getting a promotion, hitting a sales goal, building a business, going to college, getting an "A" in Biology, becoming an Eagle Scout, or simply finding some guidance and direction in life.

I've always responded to another question I'm often asked, "How do you win an Olympic Gold Medal?" I tell them "It's quite simple. You just have to be willing to commit at a level your competitors won't."

This book just might inspire you to be willing to commit to a level you didn't think you could.

Please enjoy the stories in this book. You may find yourself getting out there and making new things happen. If so, know I'm rooting for you!

Scott Hamilton
  1984 Olympic Gold Medalist
  Figure Skating

How this Book Came to Be

My dad is an Olympic athlete and a professional speaker. Ever since I was 7 years old, Dad has let me come listen to him when he speaks to different groups of people. My favorite part of his story is when he talks about fighting for your dream. How your dream is worth fighting for. It will be a struggle, but when you finally reach your dream, the victory makes it all worthwhile.

It's always like this. Dream, Struggle, Victory. ALWAYS.

No matter what your dream is, if you are willing to work hard and never give up, sooner or later you can reach your dream and have your Victory.

The Puppy Story

When I was six, I decided I wanted to have a Dachshund puppy. That was my dream. Mom and Dad said our back yard was too small for a puppy so I would have to wait until we moved to a bigger house. For two years I read books about raising and training dogs. I put pictures of dachshund puppies all over my bedroom, I talked about puppies with my parents all the time, I did not give up hope and did everything I could to show that I would be a responsible puppy owner. I went to the Houston Dog Show, I met dachshund breeders, and I learned all about how to care for dachshunds. I stayed focused and didn't quit.

That was the struggle part. But when I turned eight, even though we still had not moved to a bigger house, my parents said I had proven I could do it. And they decided to let me have a puppy. Victory!

The Colorado Story

I was born in Houston, Texas. Houston is a really big city with lots of people, lots of traffic, lots of heat and lots of mosquitoes. Our family has always dreamed of moving to Colorado. Dad did the same thing that I did when I was trying to get a puppy. He put pictures of Colorado on the walls, he read all about Colorado, he talked about Colorado all the time, we went on many Colorado vacations, we listened to John Denver music all the time, and he even put a picture of Colorado on the back cover of two of his books!

He did this for years. It seemed like we would never move to Colorado. That was the struggle part. But he didn't give up, he stayed focused and kept his hope up, and in 2010 we finally moved to Colorado. Today we live in a beautiful house out in the country with many acres to play on. Victory!

The Olympic Story

Dad competed in the sport of luge in four Olympic Games. I was not even born when Dad competed in the 1988 Calgary and the 1992 Albertville Olympics, and I was only a year old when he competed in the 2002 Salt Lake City games, so I was excited when Dad told me he was going to train to compete in the 2010 Vancouver Olympics.

For two years I have seen what dream, struggle, victory REALLY means. Dad had a big dream, he fought hard to reach it, and when he did, our whole family got to go to Vancouver to share the victory.

The Book Story

In Vancouver I got to go to the Olympic Athlete's Village and got to meet all of Dad's Olympic luge friends. I even got to meet some skiers and ice skaters. When I asked them how they got to the Olympics, their stories sounded similar. They had all had a dream, they all had to overcome some kind of obstacle — struggle — and then they finally made it, they got to enjoy their victory.

Talking to all the Olympic athletes gave me the idea of writing a book. Dad writes books, so I wanted to write one too.

Mom and Dad homeschool my brother Gracen and I. Creative writing is one of my favorite subjects. I love writing stories. When we returned from the Vancouver Olympics I told Dad I wanted to write a book filled with Olympic stories that would show people how to fight for their dreams.

My dream was to get my book written and to be an author. One day, Dad and I were eating dinner in a Mexican restaurant and I told him, "Daddy, I'm not going to be 10 years old forever. We need to get started on my book!" So we came up with a plan. We would ask 100 Olympic athletes three simple questions.

1 – When did you first get your Olympic dream?
2 – What struggle did you have to overcome?
3 – What did it feel like when you finally got your victory?

We started emailing Olympic athletes the three questions, and slowly, the answers started coming in. Everyone had struggles, but they kept their hope, they stayed focused, they didn't give up, and finally they reached their dream and got their victory.

As we read the stories we noticed that they all seemed

to fall into one of five categories: Believing in Your Dream, Planning Ahead, Committing to Your Dream, Taking Action, and Having the Character to Endure when the going got tough. So we divided the book in five parts to make it easier for the reader to learn the steps that lead to success.

I hope you like these stories, they are all very similar but they are all different. I hope that after reading these stories, you will have the courage to fight for your dreams too.

When you reach your dream and have your victory, I would love to hear about it.

Chase Your Dream!
Gabriela Gonzalez

"Everything that I've ever been able to accomplish in skating and in life has come out of adversity and perseverance."

- Scott Hamilton
1980, 1984 Figure Skating

PART ONE

Believe in Your Dream

1

Jim Craig
Ice Hockey - USA
1980 Lake Placid

Have you ever seen the movie "Miracle"? It's a very inspiring movie about the "Miracle on Ice" at the 1980 Lake Placid Olympics. The Soviet team was the best in the world and the US team was made up of college players who had only been playing together for six months. Everyone expected the Soviets to win but the Americans beat the Soviet Union in the greatest upset ever at the Olympics. Jim Craig was the goalie for the American team. He blocked 36 of 39 Soviet shots and the US won 4-3. Today Jim is a professional speaker.

Believe Your Dream is Possible

I started to dream about playing in the Olympic Games when I was in 3rd grade, almost as soon as I began to play hockey. By the way, I chose the position of goaltender because I didn't know much about hockey — the rules and all. I figured a goalie only had to know how to keep the puck out of the net.

When I was in 4th grade, my teacher noticed me sitting in the back of the class, writing and not paying attention to her instructions. She yelled out to me, "Jimmy, what are you doing?" And with confidence and conviction, I responded, "I am practicing my autograph, because I am going to play in the Olympics someday, and people are going to want my autograph."

I had talent as a hockey player, but I was also very small. I started for the varsity as a freshman, but I was only 5-1 and weighed only 110 lbs. I grew a couple inches over the next year. But in the two years beyond that, I shot up and gained weight, and was 5-10 and 180 lbs. as a senior. My team did well, and I did well. Still, no major colleges recruited me to play hockey. I attended Massasoit Community College, which had a hockey team. I listened to the advice of a mentor, Neil Higgins, who advised me to make the most of my opportunity there. I practiced and competed hard, and I was the goalie for our team which won a national community college championship.

My play at Massasoit C.C. drew the attention of Jack Parker, the coach at Boston University, a big hockey power. He offered me a full scholarship to play for the Terriers. I started out as backup goalie, and I earned a starting position, one that I maintained throughout my career at B.U. Yet even as I played well, I dealt with tremendous emotional pain because my mother was battling cancer. During my junior year, the year B.U. won the national championship, I would visit my mother every day at Massachusetts General Hospital. My mother died the summer prior to my senior year.

I made All-America as a senior, and I was selected to play on the 1980 U.S. Olympic team. Making the Olympic team was in itself a dream come true. It was my dream, and my parents' dream. Indeed, while my mother was sick and in the hospital, she made me promise that if I ever had the opportunity to represent my country in sports, I should seize that opportunity.

Winning the Gold Medal represented for me not just an individual accomplishment, but an accomplishment of supreme teamwork — an accomplishment that I shared with all those whose work, love, and devotion made it happen: my teammates, my mother and father, my coaches and other mentors, my brothers and sisters, and good friends.

Jim Craig believed his dream was possible even when he was in the 4th grade. Then he worked hard for many years to make his dream come true. I always believed I would one day have a puppy. For two years I worked hard to show my parents that I was responsible enough to have a puppy. After two years my parents got me a miniature dachshund - Biscuit. If you believe your dream is possible and if you work hard for it, you can make your dream come true.

4

"Believe the unbelievable."

- Mary Lou Retton
1984 Gymnastics

Marcelo Gonzalez
Luge - Argentina
2002 Salt Lake City

Marcelo Gonzalez is my uncle. Uncle Marcelo watched my dad compete in the 1988 Calgary and 1992 Albertville Olympics in the luge and decided he wanted to become an Olympian as well. Uncle Marcelo did not take up the sport of luge until he was over 30 years old, but he was able to qualify for the 2002 Salt Lake City Olympics. When Uncle Marcelo and my dad competed in Salt Lake, they became the first brothers to compete against each other in the men's luge in any Olympics. Today Uncle Marcelo is an architect in Houston, Texas.

It's Never too Late to Get Started

In 1988 I flew up to Canada to watch Ruben, my brother, compete in the sport of luge in the Calgary Winter Olympic Games. When I arrived in Calgary, Ruben got me a visitor's pass to the Olympic village. I had the opportunity to meet some of the other athletes from around the globe. I got to see where they stayed and trained, and to eat with them in the cafeteria. A few days later I was at the luge track watching Ruben compete. I knew little about the sport of luge and I had never seen it live. At this point I had no dreams or aspirations of ever becoming an Olympian. But each time I watched Ruben fly by me on his sled, a silly notion got stuck further and further in my head. If he can do it, then so can I. That's where it all got started for me.

Ten years later, I was at home watching the 1998 Winter Games on TV. By then, I had graduated from college with a degree in architecture and was currently working on my internship. As I watched the games, the notion that, if Ruben can do it, then so can I, started to press upon me. It wasn't the Olympic dream at this point; it was the thought that if I didn't do it now, I would regret it for the rest of my life.

The next day I went to lunch with Ruben. I asked him, what would it take to get to the Olympic Games? He explained to me the qualification requirements for the Olympics. Later he called his old coach and mentioned that I was interested in Luge. I was 33 at the time and Günther, his coach, was not excited in training someone of my age. He said, there was a training camp in Calgary starting in two weeks for new athletes. As a favor for Ruben I was allowed to attend.

Take a Chance or Else You'll Live with Regret

Two weeks later I was in Calgary. The same place where I had seen Ruben race years before. I was using my vacation time from work. I wanted to find out if this was something that I really wanted to do. I wasn't sure. I had never been on a sled. I grew up in Houston Texas, so I wasn't used to the snow. I really don't like the cold weather. But there I was. Wondering.

It was early the next morning when I got on a luge sled for the first time. Günther started me off half way down the track. He told me to relax and feel how the sled reacts to the track. He placed his shoe on the sled near my shoulder and gave me a push. I felt the sled pick up speed. I felt the wind blow over me and how the pressure built up on the curves of the track.

I loved the singularity of purpose. Architecture is so broad a subject with so many variables. On the track, it was only about getting from the top to the bottom as fast as possible. Nothing else mattered and all decisions were based on that one goal. The ride took less than a minute, but by the time I reached to bottom, I knew. I was an Olympian. In my mind and in my heart I knew that this was possible. I had caught the Olympic dream. It took less than a minute, but I could see myself walking into the Olympic stadium, in the parade of nations. At that point, I was an Olympian. I just had to put in the work to make it real.

Pay the Price - Put in the Work

There were many obstacles on the way. The first year I left my job and started my own architectural firm, GonzalezArchitects.com, so that I could work around my training and racing schedule. I had no funding so that limited the amount of training I could do. Limited training translates into more injuries on the track. The biggest obstacle was having the Olympic dream and believing that I could achieve it. Whether it took ten years of thinking about it, or one minute on the sled to make it real, I don't know. But once I had it, everything else became pragmatic. Just another step to take on the way to my dream.

In 2002 both Ruben and I competed in the Winter Olympic Games in Salt Lake City. It was all worth it, but not in the way I imagined it would be at the start. I didn't realize all the places I would see and all the people I would get to know on the way, and that many of those would become friends that would share the experience with me in the end. The journey, the good and the bad, as well as the destination became the reward. Everything from the first time Günther pushed me down the track to my final run at Salt Lake was worth it. It was all worth it.

Have you ever let the thought of failing keep you from doing something you really wanted to do? Didn't the feeling of regret make you feel sick inside? When Uncle Marcelo was watching the 1988 Winter Olympics he started thinking that if he did not at least try out the sport of luge, he would regret it later. Even though at 33 he was much older than the other athletes, he did it anyways so he would not regret it later. If you chase your dream no matter what, you will have no regrets and you will make your life an adventure.

9

Jose de Souza
Swimming - Brazil
1992 Barcelona

Jose de Souza was born in Brazil. He competed in the 1992 Olympics in swimming. He was also the World Champion and World Record Holder in the 4x100 Freestyle Relay in 1993. Jose lives in Los Angeles with his wife and two children.

What You Believe Determines what You Will Do

Growing up with Brazil's generally good weather, I fell in love with swimming as a young child. My parents tell me they had to put "floaties" on me before setting me down by a pool because I would crawl into the water without knowing how to swim. I also had bronchitis, to the point of needing to be hospitalized. When a doctor suggested my parents try swimming for my ailment (combination of exercise & humidity) they thought great — that's something he needs anyway. By the time I was 6 they begged the swimming instructor at the local club to let me try out for the lessons, that technically only allowed 7 year olds. She reluctantly agreed. The try outs would sort thru the kids into two groups; sharks and minnows. You can guess where I ended up.

Swimming for me was just fun. I loved the water, and was fortunate to have teachers and coaches that nurtured that passion without sacrificing the fun. The focus was on skills and technique. And because I was doing it at the pool with friends, I never realized I was training. It's kinda like Karate Kid's "wax on, wax off" except I loved waxing.

I started competing when I was 10, and I showed promise at an early age.

I was fortunate that my competitive nature was channeled into swimming.

Learning better technique, or eventually training harder meant I could be first, which in itself became fun. In turn, expanding the dimensions of training, from technique to endurance, range of strokes, strength, psychology, etc, became the next logical steps towards getting better. Then

11

I could beat more people and have more fun. From local competition to state level, I believe that by the time I was 12-13 years old I started to make the extension of my ambitions. I started to draw the line and make assumptions that if I did this and won state, I could (and would) do more and win nationals, and so on. And then ultimately go to the Olympics.

Believe in Yourself

The biggest struggle I had to face in the way to the Olympics was believing in myself.

I think the single most important trait of most Olympic athletes I know is their belief that they are better at their sport than everyone else. As far as I can tell, the belief that you CAN DO something is the ultimate measure, about how hard you'll train, how far you'll go, etc, to achieve your goals.

Let me give some examples. When I was a kid, I remember being extremely nervous before races. I remember peeing in my swim suit, behind the blocks, before a race. But at the same time I remember coming from behind during relay races to beat older (theoretically faster swimmers) in the lane next to me by improving multiple seconds at a time in sprint races. What I started to realize is that you have to harness your drive, your beliefs, your adrenaline - all of it - and put it all to good use. At 10 years old I had an unknown competitor tell me minutes before my race that he would beat me because his entry time was faster than mine. My response was; "You don't know what my time will be because we're going to find out in the water today." This is a small example of how you can overcome external limitations, forces, influences, or threats, by ultimately believing that you can and will transcend all of it to accomplish what you believe you can do.

My decision to leave my home, my country, my family, and move to the United States in search of better coaching, training, competition, and results, are much more extreme examples. But they are applications of the same principle. That no matter where I went, I would systematically out-train, outwork, and eventually out swim the competition. I truly BELIEVED in myself.

Never Stop Dreaming

It's funny, but I don't consider my Olympic dream to be that of what I'm most proud of. Let me explain. Over the course of one's life, you should have many dreams. And I did too.

I had a dream of first making the Olympic team. At some point I realized I didn't just want to make the team, but final. I also had dreams about winning a gold medal at the Olympics or World Championships.

I also had other dreams that have nothing to do with athletics. One dream should lead to another.

The day I made the Olympic team was one of the most memorable, happiest days of my life. Words cannot do it justice. But in retrospect, I remember it as well as the day of my first state championship at 10 years of age. And as well as the day I won a World Championship gold medal. And as well as the day I found out I received a graduate school academic scholarship. And the day my daughter, then my son, were born.

I did not achieve all of my goals. But I achieved many. And I discovered along the way that the journey is just as important as the destination.

I know several gold medal winners that didn't appreciate their journey, even their win, as much as I think they should. That may be because their goals were even higher or that they also wanted the record, or that they hated the training that it took to get there — I don't know. But I think my biggest sense of joy from making that dream come true, was my appreciation for what I had done to get there, and that I had learned to never stop learning. To never stop dreaming.

Jose de Souza lives his life from one dream to another. He believes that if he works hard enough he can reach his dreams. He also likes to have fun along the way so that he will enjoy his journey. My dad always tells me that if I work hard and have fun as I chase my dreams, I'll make my life an adventure.

"He who is not courageous enough to take risks will accomplish nothing in life."

- Muhammad Ali
1960 Boxing

Roberto Benitez
Boxing - USA
2004 Athens

Roberto Benitez was born in New York. He was a National Golden Gloves Champion and went on to compete in the 2004 Olympics. Then he became a profesional boxer. Roberto lives in Florida.

Take On Big Challenges

I received my first Olympic Dream opportunity in 2000 but came up short qualifying for the Games. Missing the Olympics felt terrible, but I decided to train for the 2004 Olympics. I trained hard and four years later I was ranked number one in the country in my division. I then won the Olympic qualifying tournament to make the team. After missing the 2000 Olympics, the 2004 Olympic team felt like breathing a breath of fresh air.

The biggest struggle I faced on the way to the Olympics was when I moved up to another weight division just a few months before qualifying for the Olympic team. I had been dominating my old division for years and I had to move up to another category that was more competitive. Many people felt I would not be able to adjust or outdo my new competition since there were bigger guys. I had to prove myself to all the boxing insiders and show them I was a special fighter. I adapted well and still dominated by defeating the top ranked fighters in that division and still made the team. Whenever other people don't believe in you, ignore them, follow your heart, work extra hard, and prove them wrong.

Realizing my Olympic dream was redemptive. It proved to myself that I could accomplish anything as long as I believed in myself and was willing to put in the work. Accomplishing this dream made me grow mentally and spiritually and gave me a substantial amount of confidence.

The most important message I would share with everyone is that you must always have faith. You also need to be willing to make sacrifices if you want to see your dreams come into fruition. If you build it, it will come. If you begin building your dream with hard work then that dream will eventually come true. It does not matter if it takes years or months because building your masterpiece takes patience as you learn from your mistakes. No matter how hard you have to work for your dream, when you reach it, you will know it was worth it.

Most people would have quit after training four long years and missing the Olympic cut. Roberto refused to give up on his dream. He not only decided to commit the next four years to train for the Olympics, but he did so by fighting at a heavier division. Champions don't let setbacks keep them down. Boxers know better than anyone that when you get knocked down you need to get back in the fight right away. Be like a fighter. When life knocks you down, don't quit. Get back up and fight for your dream.

Daniela Meuli
Snowboarding - Switzerland
2002 Salt Lake City; 2006 Torino

Daniela Meuli is a Swiss snowboarder. She was the World Champion in 2005 and won the Gold Medal at the 2006 Torino Olympics in the parallel giant slalom.

Trust Your Heart

When I was 6 years old I was a big fan of Pirmin Zurbriggen, a great Swiss ski racer and Olympic Champion. I watched him every time he raced and of course I saw him compete in the Olympics. I was amazed and for me it was clear: "I want do the same and I want be an Olympic Champion like Pirmin!" From this moment on I had the Dream to become Olympic Champion and I never let this dream die! I tried a lot of different sports like ski, track and field, soccer, swimming, basketball, judo and some others. When I was 14 years old I tried snowboarding. As soon as I did, I knew I had found my sport. I was infected with the Carving Virus. I loved racing against others, speed became my passion and especially I loved the parallel racing system used in snowboarding. As the years went by, my Olympic dream came closer and closer.

The most important thing that I learned on my way to becoming Olympic Champion was to believe in my own intuition. I learned that it is not important what other people think about you, and it's not important what others think about how you train. What's important is that you believe in yourself and that you believe in your plan. I always followed my heart and payed little attention to what others said.

Another thing that I learned was how to work with the media. At the beginning of my career working with the media was a big problem for me. The media made me very nervous and I was actually thinking about my answers to the journalists even during the competition. As you can imagine, that was terrible, because I was not focusing on my snowboard training. Instead of this I was thinking about the interviews after the competition. But finally I find a solution for this problem. I prepared a lot of standard answers for the journalists most common questions and in the evening before the competition days I prepared some answers for the interview right after the race. So I was prepared for everything and my head and body were ready to be focused on my "competition work."

Competing in the Olympics was unbelievable! I had always thought that when sports champions said the words "I can't realize what I've done," they could not have been telling the truth. But I have to say that I felt the same way. Of course when I was standing on the Podium at Olympics it was fantastic and I was so happy. But I did not realize what I had done until ten days later. After the Olympics, we had our next Word Cup Race in Russia. One day before our race I was jogging alone around some hills in the Russian countryside. I had to stop jogging because I realized: "Oh my God, I reached my biggest dream, the dream that I had since I was a little girl. This dream came true and I am Olympic Champion!!" It was a very emotional moment for me and I could not stop the tears of joy from rolling down my cheeks.

There are always people out there that have opinions about what you should be doing. When my Dad decided to take up the sport of luge, a lot of people told him he was crazy. When Daniela was training for the Olympics, there were people that thought she should train differently. Daniela was strong and she focused on listening to her heart. By listening to her coaches and her heart, Daniela was able to focus on her best path and she was able to realize her Olympic dream.

"My doctor told me I would never walk again. My mother told me I would. I believed my mother."

- Wilma Rudolph
1960 Track

Julia Siparenko
Alpine Skiing - Ukraine
2002 Salt Lake City; 2006 Torino

Julia Siparenko competed in alpine skiing at the 2002 Salt Lake City Olympics. Today she is the Secretary General of the Ukraine Ski Federation, the governing body of the sport of ski in Ukraine.

24

Get Started and Don't Quit

I remember the moment clearly. I was 15 years old. On that remarkable season of 1995 – my last in the children's competitions – I took part in the National Championship. We were racing on the famous Trostyan slope in Ukraine and I won the Giant Slalom race. My Coach and I were happy, but, what really was surprising and even a bit embarrassing for me, was that many, many other people – not only from my team, but also others and even judges – also have shared those emotions. Afterwards, upon coming back home, we had a small celebration party at home and my coach said to my Mom, "Well, our next goal is the 1998 Nagano Olympics." And that was it. That's how my Olympic dream came to be.

The biggest challenge on the way to the Olympics was that Ukraine did not have a very effective athlete development system. Ukraine did not have any distinguished results, as World Cup, European Cup or Championships medals. These are the only things that carry weight and get support in our sport system. I was not one of the strongest alpine skiers in the world and the only way to get to Olympics under such circumstances was to be the best in your country. Unfortunately I failed to become the Ukrainian leader before Nagano-98. I desperately hoped to get there and it was a great frustration. But I was determined to continue competing. Remarkably one month after the Nagano Olympics I confirmed my first place. There were many struggles and challenges afterwards, as back problems, lack of training opportunities, lack of proper equipment. I always tried to do my job the best possible way and remembered the goal. I did not focus on the struggles. Instead, I drew strength from my goal.

Finally, in 2002, I was able to compete in the Salt Lake City Olympics. I kept training and was able to compete in the 2006 Torino Olympics. My family, especially my Mom was always supporting me. When you have to struggle for a dream and fight the challenges, you start learning how to win even before the competition itself. The harder the struggle, the more precious becomes this "win" – to reach your dream.

Realizing my Olympic dream filled me with total happiness. I was totally penetrated with the fact that I had actually done it. As usual, there were a thousand of small organizational problems, but all of them were easily overcome, because I simply focused on the dream. Everything felt different. It was as if everything I did were filled with the color of my dream.

What made me even more confident and joyous, were the many cheers and good luck wishes during the Salt Lake City Olympics. I never imagined that so many people would support and cross their fingers for me. This sharing of the feeling makes the realization of dream much more intensive. Because you realize that it was all a team effort. I'm really grateful to everybody, who helped me in different ways on the way to my Olympic dream.

There are always challenges on the road to your dream. Julia was a great skier but her country did not have a good skiing development system. Like many athletes, Julia faced injuries and setbacks - like missing out on competing in the Nagano Olympics. But she focused on her dream and kept training. Julia's strength to overcome her challenges came from her dream. Focus on your dream. Get started and don't quit. And before long you will realize your dream just like Julia did.

*"I am building a fire, and everyday
I train, I add more fuel.
At just the right moment,
I light the match."*

*- Mia Hamm
1996, 2000, 2004 Soccer*

PART TWO

Plan Ahead

Marilyn King
Pentathlon - USA
Munich 1972; Montreal 1976

Marilyn King competed in the Pentathlon (100 meter hurdles, shot put, high jump, long jump and 800 meters) in the 1972 and 1976 Olympics. While she was training for the 1980 Olympics, she injured her back in a car wreck and was bed-ridden for five months. She spent that time watching films of pentathletes and visualizing herself winning the Pentathlon. Even though she missed months of training (Marilyn typically trained 6-8 hours every day), she was able to qualify in the top three for the 1980 Olympics. She is the founder of Beyond Sports, an organization that teaches people how to reach their goals by using passion, vision, and action.

See It, Believe It, and then Do It

With few exceptions, Olympians are ordinary people - ordinary people who have accomplished extraordinary things. I should know.

I am one of those ordinary Olympians who wanted to understand why I had been able to accomplish so much when I knew that my athletic skills were only slightly above average.

After six years of soul searching, I decided to meet with other Olympians and ask them why they had been successful. We gathered Winter and Summer Olympians, team and individual sport athletes, men and women, medalists and non-medalists. Regardless of our sport, nationality or final placing, we had all accomplished things that were "unimaginable" to most people. The purpose of our weekend gatherings was to determine what we had in common that allowed us to achieve at that level.

Our weekends in the mountains were the opportunity to brainstorm all the elements we could think of that were even remotely related to our ability to achieve at the Olympian level. When we refined our lists, the elements fell easily into four categories: body (taking action), mind (visualizing), spirit (passion), and "other."

Our largest category was the mental skills area. Athletes have always known that in order to accomplish any lofty goal, you must have a crystal clear image of that goal and keep it uppermost in your mind.

Dare to Imagine that You Can Reach Your Dream

We know that by maintaining that image, the "how-to" steps necessary for the realization of the goal will begin to emerge spontaneously. Initially, none of these athletes knew exactly what it would take to become an Olympian, but with the goal in mind, the steps to achieving it became readily apparent. If you cannot imagine the goal, the "how-to" steps will never emerge and you'll never do it. The first step to any achievement is to dare to imagine you can do it.

Mental rehearsal was another important skill. It is employed prior to any performance literally to mentally rehearse the precise details of that performance to help its execution.

Get Passionate About Your Dream

While mental skills play an interesting and important role in superior performance, it is the emotions or spirit that give Olympians and other peak performers the energy to do what it takes to succeed. Most people feel they lack the will power and discipline that it takes to succeed at a high level in any field; they see those as attributes belonging to "others." *What looks like will power and discipline from the outside is really passion on the inside.* These athletes are people who were passionate about their pursuits. It was that gut level, emotional involvement that gave them that enviable energy and drive. They knew exactly what they wanted and were determined to get it. Being passionate about something unlocks all the energy and creativity necessary to achieve the goal.

Take Action

The third category is the physical. The surprise in this area was that it was the shortest list. It became apparent that while the physical was important, it was not superior physical skills that were a major factor. Far more important were the mental and emotional categories.

Many Olympians acknowledged that there were significant numbers of athletes with superior physical attributes who never made an Olympic team. The key in this category was the physical act of doing something every day in the service of the goal.

Build a Dream Team

In the other category were items that did not fit anywhere else. Of these, what stands out in my mind is parental support. One Olympian summed it up best when she stated, "What I got from my parents was the notion that I could achieve anything I set my mind to." As I looked around the room, all heads were nodding in agreement. I believe the single most important thing parents can give their children is the belief that all things are possible to the passionate and persistent.

The Olympians who gathered in the mountains of Northern California to complete this work were unanimous in their conclusions. The major lesson is that the skills common to these high performers are not special gifts or talents, but instead innate abilities that can be awakened in each and every human being.

Dad taught me that whenever I have a goal or a dream I should always take the same steps. Imagine what it will feel like when I make my dream come true, put pictures of my dream where I can see them all the time, let myself get excited about reaching my dream, and get to work doing whatever needs to be done to reach my dream. It's pretty simple, but it works. It will work for you too.

John Naber
Swimming - USA
Montreal 1976

John Naber is one of America's most successful Olympic champions. He was America's most highly decorated Olympian at the 1976 Games in Montreal earning four gold medals in swimming, each in world record time. Naber became the first swimmer in history to earn two individual medals on the same day of Olympic competition, and earned the Sullivan Award as America's top amateur athlete of 1977. John Naber is a sports broadcaster and a speaker.

Plan and Prepare to Win

When I was a kid, I was visiting Olympia, Greece, with my family. The tour guide told us about the Ancient Olympic Games and how they were designed to honor the gods. Then, he mentioned the "Hall of Shame" where cheaters got statues carved in their likeness, so they would always be embarrassed. I liked the idea of a sporting event dedicated to sportsmanship instead of "victory at any cost" so I told my mother, "I am going to be an Olympian, someday!" She asked me, "In what sport?" I had no idea but eventually swimming became my sport.

My biggest challenge on the way to the Olympics was an injury I sustained right before the Olympic Trials. Three months before the 1972 Olympic Trials, I double- and triple-bounced on the diving board, so when I dove off the board, I literally missed the water (and broke my collar bone in the process). On the way to the hospital, I knew that my bone was broken, but I was already planning how to keep training without getting wet. Eventually, I spend six weeks walking the side of the pool, along-side my coach, studying the sport and what swimmers can do to get better, faster. Within two months I was back in the water, and I was turning in times that were faster than my previous best. At the Trials, I just missed making the team, but I knew that I was destined to make the next team. As soon as the 1972 Trials were over, I immediately turned my sights on 1976.

Making the 1976 Olympic team was a major accomplishment, but I had been dreaming about the Olympic gold medal races for a long time. I knew that I could win the gold, but I didn't know if I would win the gold. When I looked up at the scoreboard and saw that I had broken the world record, I felt something like relief and joy. My greatest satisfaction was watching how proud my Mom and Dad were of me, and receiving a warm "bear hug" from my normally stoic coach.

Most people would have quit on their Olympic dream if they had broken a collarbone right before the Olympic Trials. John Naber took advantage of his time off by spending six weeks studying the swimmers while walking alongside his coach. John learned new techniques and planned on how he would use them. Afterwards he was faster than ever before. Dad always tells my brother Gracen and I to plan ahead. When you get knocked down, plan ahead. Figure out a way to come back stronger.

*"I didn't set out to beat the world;
I just set out to do my absolute best."*

- Al Oerter
1956, 1960, 1964, 1968 Discus

Khadevis Robinson
800 Meters - USA
Athens 2004

Khadevis "KD" ran the 800 meters for the US in the 2004 Athens Olympics. Khadevis is the head cross country coach at UNLV and the president of the Track and Field Athletes Association. He's also a professional speaker.

Learn from Your Mistakes

In 2000, I went into the USA Outdoor Olympic trials as one of the favorites to make the Olympic team. Yet, the week leading up to the trials I got a bit sick. I was not very sick but had some symptoms similar to bad allergies. I tried my best not to get too worried or concerned and had actually ran fairly well throughout the rounds, yet in the final, coming into the final 100, I found myself in 3rd place and got caught before the line and ended up getting fourth place. This being the case, I was extremely focused and prepared in 2004. I ran a nearly perfect race on that day and I made sure I ran it properly so that I could make the Olympic team. It was an awesome experience considering what I had gone through four years prior. I realized my first Olympic dream first in Eugene, Oregon at the Olympic trials, then in Athens, Greece in 2004.

Focus on the Present

My biggest struggle on the way to the Olympics was getting over my earlier failures and mistakes. I had to really focus on the here and now and not get distracted on things that had happened in the past. Not only the experience of barely missing out on making the team four years earlier but everything I had gone through throughout my life. I was literally born and lived on the wrong side of the tracks. All of my self limiting, self defeating, and self doubt would always come back when I encountered any big obstacle. From all of the years of individuals telling me I would never graduate from High School. From the times people told me I would not live to reach the age of 19. From reading all the statistics that said individuals like myself were not supposed to grow up and be successful. All of these "shadows" would always haunt me. They were like weeds in a garden. You know, you plant the fruit, vegetables, and flowers, but the weeds just grow. I had to overcome all of these negative thoughts. I had to realize that winning is not always about coming in first place or coming home with the most marbles. Winning is knowing that you gave your all and had nothing left once you were finished. I realized that "Major things happen in Minor moments" and this was my moment. I committed to give it my all and I was able to make the 2004 Olympic team.

Making the Olympic team is a feeling that is hard to describe. It's as if you are in a dream. You are there but you are not there. The interesting thing is it felt that much more rewarding because of everything I had to go through. I think if it would have been easy for me to make the team maybe I would not have valued it as much. Yet, because it was so hard, making it was that much more rewarding. I found out that reaching a goal is not necessarily as important as what you become in pursuit of a goal. There is "Power in Pursuit" as Les Brown would say. I gained much needed power in my pursuit of my Olympic dream. I also learned that reaching your dream should be difficult. You see, Tony Dungy said it best when he said "Success is uncommon, therefore not to be enjoyed by common man. I'm looking for uncommon people." I feel that going through everything I went through is an uncommon thing and you have to be uncommon to be willing to put yourself through this. I am definitely glad I did.

Imagine working as hard as you can on a goal to the point of which you do not know if you will ever achieve it, and you are right on the brink of giving up, only to finally achieve it. Imagine that feeling! Then multiply it times 100.

That is what it was like to finally have my dream come true!

Khadevis teaches that our mind is like a garden. You plant nice vegetables but weeds always grow. If you want a good garden you need to pull the weeds and take care of your vegetables. A bad thought in your mind. A thought that wants to keep you from your dream, pull the weed. Get rid of that thought and focus on your dream.

Michael Binzer
Cross Country Skiing - Denmark
Albertville 1992;
Lillehammer 1994; Nagano 1998

Michael Binzer was born in Greenland and competed in cross country skiing for Denmark. He is a graduate of Wharton Business College and is the CEO of Air Greenland.

Team Up with Winners

As a 15 year old – growing up in remote Greenland, I decided to be a skier with a dream of one day participating in the Olympic Winter Games. Greenland did not have a strong ski training program and it was too far from all the top ski training areas. Thus I had to move to Norway, which I did when I turned 17 years old. At that time I chose to study at the University of Oslo in order to pursue a full time career as a cross-country skier, but with the option of also pursuing a University degree.

The biggest challenge I faced on the road to the Olympics was finding the proper financing and training opportunities to reach my goals. So I made a "battle-plan" in order to find corporate sponsorships. When you are focused on your dream you develop the attitude that no matter what challenges you face, you will find a way.

At the age of 22 years old I reached my goal and participated in the 1992 Olympics in Albertville. This was a fantastic experience and I decided to keep on going for the next Olympics in Lillehammer 1994, where I also competed. My goals got bigger and the feeling of achievement – on a personal level – felt as conquering yourself again and again. I also had the joy of participating in Nagano 1998 – before I had to end my career as a skier. However many hours training in mountains, forest and cities of the world have taught me one thing: shoot for the stars – and you'll reach the moon.

I have used the lessons I learned on the road to the Olympics in my business life. I have always loved aviation, and today I am proud to be the CEO of Air Greenland.

In order to reach your dream, you may have to move to another city. Or like Michael, to another country. Just because Greenland did not have a strong ski training program, did not mean Michael could not become an Olympic skier. He just moved to where the best coaches were. When Dad decided to compete in the sport of luge, he lived in Houston. That did not stop him. Dad simply spent his winters in Lake Placid and in Europe to learn how to luge. My great great grandparents moved from Italy to Argentina at the turn of the century seeking more opportunity. Sixty years later, my grandparents moved from Argentina to the US for the same reason. Be willing to move to wherever the people who can help you reach your dreams live.

*"If you fail to prepare,
you're prepared to fail."*

*- Mark Spitz
1972 Swimming*

Annette Huygens-Tholen
Beach Volleyball - Australia
Sydney 2000

Annette Huygens-Tholen (now Annette Lynch) is using all of her Olympic experience to teach others how to reach their goals. She's the author of "Success Beyond Sport," a personal coach and a speaker.

Find a Path to Your Dream

We were standing in the tunnel waiting to march in, listening to hear our country being called. The excitement and anticipation built within us, until finally they called "Australia!" My beach volleyball partner and I grabbed each other's hands, celebrating this moment. We've done it, we're here!

It was one of the proudest moments in my life. My childhood dream was to go the Olympics. I was a young gymnast, 10 years old, when Nadia Comaneci wowed the world with her perfection during the 1976 Olympic Games in Montreal.

Those were the first Olympic Games I took an interest in and really understood, particularly the gymnastics competition. I also recall being absolutely mesmerized by the opening and closing ceremonies. That was the moment my dream began. I would be a part of that opening ceremony and someday compete in the Olympics.

I was only fifteen when I was advised that I could no longer compete in gymnastics. My back was damaged and my dream of going to the Olympics was shattered. My initial reaction was devastation. Gymnastics had honed my discipline and had fueled my ambition to succeed. Without it, I was lost and miserable.

Even at that young age, I was instinctively in the habit of finding other ways to reach my goals. I started asking myself questions like "If I can't do gymnastics, what other sport could I participate in? What sport would I possibly excel in? How can I still go to the Olympics?"

Meanwhile I had also started playing volleyball at high school; though at this stage it was just for fun. It was also time to consider my career and I decided to study physiotherapy at my University. I was thinking that "here's another way I could get to the Olympic Games...if not as an athlete, then as a therapist." My dream remained alive and burning in my mind.

I continued to play indoor volleyball progressing to the state team and eventually to the Australian team. I started playing beach volleyball in 1987 as a summer sport and by 1992/93 it had became a major passion for me. Not being particularly tall, it was a sport suited to my athleticism and agility.

When beach volleyball was announced as a medal sport for the Olympic Games in Atlanta, I finally had a real chance of becoming an Olympian. I had enjoyed success the previous summer on the Australian Beach Volleyball tour with a team ranking of number two. I decided to step down from the Indoor program and focus entirely on a beach career.

By end of 1994 I was ranked 8th in the world with my beach volleyball partner. I was on track to qualify for Atlanta, but my partner had other ideas. She didn't want to just qualify, she wanted to win a medal and she decided she could do this with another partner. I was shocked at the break-up but I knew I needed to keep going. I moved interstate to pursue a new partnership and we failed to qualify for the 1996 Olympic Games. My ex-partner went on to win a Bronze medal in Atlanta while I sat at home watching.

I was still focused on getting to the Olympics though, so I moved cities again found a new partner and played a couple of years with her on the World Tour before she too thought it was time to play with someone else. My next partner lasted just four months and the coaches decided she would be better partnered with another girl.

Finally I partnered up with Sarah Straton - we were two players who had endured through various partner break-ups and amongst Australian teams were considered the 'least likely to succeed.' We thought otherwise and were determined to make the 2000 Olympic team.

It wasn't easy, and we had our own internal challenges including a brief split half-way through but ultimately we realized out best option was to stick together. Persistence and believing in our dream led to us walking through that tunnel at the opening ceremony in Sydney 2000 in front of 100,000 fans.

My greatest moment was playing the game of my life the next day before 10,000 people at Bondi Beach. I felt unbeatable at the net, and served several aces in the game against the 2nd ranked team in the world. We lost in a very tight encounter, and 2 days later we lost again to be out of the competition. I did record an Olympics record for fastest serve during that game, so I left with some pride at how I played this game and how I made this dream happen.

It all starts with a dream!

Annette, had an Olympic dream but had to find the right path for her. Annette knew that she would find way as long as she refused to give up. Dad's story is similar. He knew he could not become an Olympian playing soccer, so he found a sport that became his vehicle to the Olympics - the luge. God puts a dream in your heart and he gives you all the gifts you need to realize your dream. You just have to develop your gifts, work your heart out, and refuse to quit until you find the path that leads to your dream.

Mateusz Kusznierewicz
Sailing - Poland
Atlanta 1996; Sydney 2000; Athens 2004; Beijing 2008; London 2012

Mateusz's has a connection with boats from even before the time he was born as his parents got married on a Yacht. From the time he was three years old, his parents took Mateusz sailing. In 1999, the International Sailing Federation awarded Mateusz with the ISAF Sailor of the Year award. That year he was also named the most popular athlete in Poland. When he's not sailing, Mateusz enjoys playing tennis, golf and traveling.

Look Ahead and Plan Ahead

I started my sailing adventure in 1984, at first I didn't think about the Olympics. It was not until seven years later, right before the Barcelona Olympics, that I started to feel the spirit of Olympics and in 1992 I started training for the next Olympics. I followed all the regatas (sailing races) and had my favorite competitors. Back then I looked up to Canadian and Spanish sailors. I paid close attention to what the best sailors did. Everyone thought that the winner would be Canadian, meanwhile Spanish sailor won the gold and Canadian was 10th. From that time I started to see myself as an Olympic sailor.

Sailing is a very complicated and complex discipline. You have to focus on your physical condition, equipment, technique and meteorology. You have to train with a coach, and a teammate. Training for sailing takes a lot of time and the lack of it is the biggest challenge, so much to do and so little time. For that reason, good organization and concentration are the two most important factors in becoming a good sailor. Planning and forseeing are crucial. Not only what will happen next day, but also, next week, month. You have to also be a good strategist. Proper use of your free time is also very important. The best way to keep your body fit and in good shape for sailing is sleep. You must give your mind time to rest sometimes. My way to relax is also sport. I like spending time playing golf, rollerskating and jogging. I love what I do and I like improving my skills and it is my inner drive and that gives me motivation.

Many years of planning, strategizing, training and competing culminated in the Olympics. Competing in the Olympics was a moment of huge satisfaction and euphoria.

I must admit that it was also very fullfiling, I was happy not only for myself but also for my familly, fans and for those who make up for my success. After a month I already wanted to sail, train and set up the new goals, I started to think about next Olympics. One dream leads to another.

Mateusz had an Olympic dream but he understood that dreaming is not enough. You need to plan ahead, strategize, manage your time, listen to your coaches, and focus on your dream. By doing those things, Mateusz has already competed in five Olympics. Dad had to plan ahead as well. He picked the sport of luge because it fit him well, but then he had to plan his training around school and work. He also had to save enough money so that he could go luging when the season started. Dad always teaches us the importance of not just having one plan, but of having a Plan A, a Plan B, a Plan C and so on, in case Plan A does not work out. By thinking ahead and planning ahead you can make your dreams come true as well.

Bernhard Russi
Alpine Skiing - Switzerland
Sapporo 1972; Innsbruck 1976

Russi currently serves as the chairman of the FIS (International Ski Federation) Alpine Committee and is a FIS technical advisor for downhill course design. Beginning with the 1988 Calgary Olympics, Russi has been the designer of the Olympic downhill courses. He also serves as a commentator for alpine ski racing on Swiss television.

The Power of Visualization

As a young boy, I dreamt of the Olympics, but was not thinking to participate myself one day. I was just fascinated about the greatness of sport, about the spirit, about the power of sport over all the problems in the world, like politics, race, religions and cultures.

Then, on the opening speech of a training camp five years prior to Sapporo 1972, our Coach Adolf Ogi, placed a poster of the Sapporo Olympics on the wall, and said: "You can be there, if you do the right thing....and a little bit more!"

My biggest challenge on the way to the Olympics was placing the idea of an Olympic race correctly in my mind. To imagine years before, what would happen at that moment, to imagine the additional pressure, to anticipate in my head and brain all the special things which would happen around the games. To live with the thought, that this race day will not be something normal. Something I needed to be ready for. Picturing in my mind exactly what that day would be like was my biggest challenge. But by doing so I was ready when the big day came.

Because I was racing with the bib number 4, after I had finished my racing run, I had to wait in the finish area almost one hour, until all the other skiers raced before I was sure to be Olympic Champion. Being an Olympic Champion did not hit me until I was all alone in my room later that day. At that point, total happiness came to me. All the pressure of the mounts, days, hours and minutes before this Olympic race came out. I was first screaming as loud as I could, then I lay on my bed and cried for 20 minutes.

The next unforgettable moment was the Medal ceremony. I was surrounded with all my friends and family, and I felt like I was surrounded by my whole country. I couldn't hold back my tears. The power was gone and another power took place, the power of an Olympic Gold Medal!

Bernhard pictured his Olympic race for years. Visualizing what it would be like and what it would feel like helped him be ready on race day. Dad did the same thing. For years he pictured what it would feel like to walk in the Opening Ceremonies. That picture gave Dad the strength to overcome the challenges on the road to the Olympics. For years I pictured and imagined what it would be like to have a puppy. As a family, we pictured what it would be like to live in Colorado. You can do the same thing. Picture what it will be like when you realize your dream. Visualizing your dream is like running your own personal "Coming Attractions" of what the movie of your future life will be like.

*"If you don't have confidence,
you'll always find a way not to win."*

*- Carl Lewis
1984, 1988, 1992, 1996 Track*

Darrin Steele
Bobsled - USA
Nagano 1998; Salt Lake City 2002

Darrin Steele, is the CEO of the U.S. Bobsled & Skeleton Federation. Steele was a decathlete at Eastern Illinois University, where he earned bachelor's and master's degrees in economics. His favorite moment in the sport was when the US bobsled team won three medals at the Salt Lake City Olympics in 2002. Outside of bobsledding, Darrin enjoys reading, basketball, golf, and spending time with his wife and three children.

Prepare for the Worst

I first dreamed of competing in the Olympics as I watched Bruce Jenner win the 1976 Montreal Olympic decathlon when I was 7 years old. It was a pipe dream until I earned a bronze medal at the World University Games in 1993 in the decathlon. That's when I got serious about training. Bobsled was not even in my mind until after the 1996 Olympic Track and Field Trials. When I failed to make the team, I accepted an invitation to try bobsledding and I was a natural at it. I never looked back and make the Olympic bobsled team the next season.

The biggest struggle I had on my way to the Olympic was fighting injuries. It was a continuation of the same issue I faced in track and field and I didn't want the same thing to happen to me in bobsled. I became a student of my own body and muscles and taught myself how to recognize injuries before they occurred and learned the discipline to back off my training when I felt something. As a result I was able to stay healthy and therefore able to have a full training cycle without injuries. It is really difficult to force yourself to back off training when you are trying to be the best in the world, but my ability to do that helped me to make the Olympic team.

Competing in the Olympics felt like I was dreaming. I was walking on air and I thought about all the hard work and the struggles and I was really emotional. It was greater than I ever imagined.

Dad says that life is tough so we need to be tougher. You will have ups and downs so you must be mentally prepared

61

to bounce back when life knocks you down. Injuries are just a part of sports. Darrin understood this and learned how to become aware of how his body felt so that he could take care of his injuries before they became too big to handle. It's like my Dad likes to say, "Hope for the best but prepare for the worst."

*"A good plan violently executed
right now is better than a perfect
plan executed next week."*

*- George Patton
1912 Modern Pentathlon*

Sam Hall
Diving - USA
Rome 1960

Sam Hall was born in Dayton, Ohio. He won the silver medal in diving at the 1960 Rome Olympics. Sam is a former member of the Ohio House of Representatives. Sam has climbed mountains and explored the world through his work with relief and rescue missions.

See It in Your Mind

When I was a kid, my Dad took our family every winter for vacations at a Florida hotel where all the world-class swimmers and divers used to stay for year-round training. I would watch them for hours at a time, especially the divers with their tip-toed poise and long leaps off the high board. I loved the way they hugged themselves into balls and seemed suspended in the air for a long second before they stretched out and started down to make nearly splash-less entries into the blue water. I started copying the form I saw at the hotel pool. By the time I was fourteen and back in school in Dayton I was getting really good, thanks to practicing three or four hours every day. I wanted to be the best diver ever and the Olympics became my goal.

I always believed that I was destined to win because my diving coach at Ohio State, Mike Peppe, made it simple for me and my training. I worked out 3 times a day. During each practice he instructed me to think prior to each dive that the stands, which were empty, were full. So even at my very first workout, on the first day of my three per day workouts - in my mind, the stands were full and 7 tough judges sat in their respective seats. In my mind, I performed each dive in front of a packed house. If I missed a dive (in front of the full imaginary stands of people and 7 rough judges) I was not to repeat the missed dive, instead, I had to make up for the previous dive by excelling on the next dive. Practicing like that made me sharp. Coach Peppe, made it even more simple - he would say, "Sam, it's simple. Up on one and down on two." He would also say, "Take it up, spin it and drop it." Coach Peppe was ahead of his time...he would tell me, "Run through your list of dives at least 10 times each day and DO NOT REPEAT A DIVE IF YOU MISSED ONE, CONTINUE ON. This Muscle Memory is the key. Keep doing it over and over."

Although the Olympic trials in Detroit made me the favorite to take the gold medal, I had to settle for a silver medal in Rome when my feet brushed the board on my last dive and Gary Tobian from USC beat me with a great performance. After all the hard work I had put in, all of the support and pushing my dad had given me, and after Sports Illustrated and other magazines rated me the best diver in the world, second was a crushing blow. God knows my dad wanted me to give him that gold medal and doing that would have been the best thing that ever happened to me, but now I was second best. I didn't know how my dad would take it or what he'd say when he made his way poolside, but he clamped me in a bear hug and whispered, "I'm so proud of you," and then hugged Gary Tobian too with the tears flowing all around. That's when I knew that the whole Olympic episode would glow brighter in my memory than any mere bronze, silver or gold.

When I stood on the block with the stars and stripes above my head, I felt ten feet tall and the national anthem sent shivers down my spine. Ever since then I haven't been able to watch any Olympic ceremony on TV without tears in my eyes. The 1960 games hooked me on living a life filled with challenges and excitement. Going head to head with athletes from all over the world and making friends from Europe and South America and Asia and Africa - those things were burned in my memory. I wanted the rest of my life to be that intense.

Sam's coach was ahead of his time. He helped Sam become a champion by teaching him how to visualize the perfect dive. Dad did the same thing when he trained for the luge. He could only take five or six luge runs a day but he took hundreds or luge runs in his mind. If you constantly picture what you want to happen, eventually you can start making it happen.

Catherine Garceau
Synchronized Swimming - Canada
Sydney 2000

Catherine Garceau is an Olympic medalist, the author of "Swimming Out of Water," and a keynote speaker. Catherine helps women with emotional eating, and binge eating solutions through her personal coaching program.

Learn from Others

In 1988, when Carolyn Waldo won the double Gold at the Seoul Olympics in Synchronized Swimming, I was mesmerized by her beauty and strength in the water. I watched the recording of her performance over and over. It was Carolyn's victory in Seoul that planted the Olympic seed in my mind and heart. In 1997, after already 8 years of intense training, I made the National A Team and started competing against the top teams worldwide. In 1999, I moved from Montreal, my home town, to Toronto, to be with the team.

A work ethic and a toned physique were the assets I brought to the team. My weakness was a lack of physical endurance, which prevented me from performing our 4 to 5 routines with technical accuracy from start to finish. I hadn't realized how important it was to see my performance and myself in a more positive light, and to stop being so overly hard on myself, in order to improve my performance. So, with the help of sports psychologists, I began a quest to develop a much stronger inner game, which is where success really stems from.

In 1999, one of our last competitions before the final Olympic team selection was the Pan Am Games. Nine swimmers would make the cut. I didn't make it. I was shocked and devastated, and my efforts to gain a stronger mindset seemed useless, until I decided to look for an opportunity in this setback. I wondered if there was a gift in being a spectator at the Pan Am Games. There had to be. So, I observed and noted everything I could of my competitors and discovered ways I could gain a competitive advantage. I was turning this major disappointment into an exciting turning point.

69

Less than 2 months later, I performed at my best, and earned a spot to swim both short and long programs at the Sydney Olympics. My Olympic dream was finally realized. I cherish many memories from my Olympic journey, including our Bronze Medal. After the Olympics, I kept training towards the 2004 Olympic Games, but was stopped in my tracks due to a stubborn eating disorder and depression. Ten years later, I'm happy to say that I feel equally proud of my healing journey as I do of my Olympic journey. "Olympians in spirit" are found in all walks of life. With heart, commitment and discipline, I believe that everyone can tap into the hero within, overcome the greatest challenges, and create miracles for themselves and others.

Catherine was too hard on herself and that kept her from performing at her best. Fortunately, she was smart enough to work with sports psychologists who taught her how to develop a winning mindset. Catherine used her new winning mindset to realize her Olympic dream. Dad always relies on other people's knowledge to get where he wants to go. He likes to say, "If you have to cross a minefield, it makes sense to follow someone who has already crossed it." Find people who can help you get where you want to go.

Greg Sun
Bobsled - Trinidad & Tobago
Lillehammer 1994; Nagano 1998;
Salt Lake City 2002

Greg Sun competed in three Winter Olympics in the bobsled representing his native Trinidad & Tobago. He has a Masters in Sports Science and works for Washington State University.

Master the Basics

In 1991, I arrived in Alberta Canada with a friend of mine to help him drive around their bobsleigh athletes in preparation for their World Cup race. It was my first trip North, as I was currently studying at the University of Idaho, which was a 10 hour drive to Calgary. My introduction to Canada was the 30° F high temperature which did not vary much for the 2 weeks I spent there. Something caught my eye when I went to get the rental van. It was plugged into an outlet and I was wondering, was this was a electric vehicle? I asked the attendant, and after a few chuckles at my question; he explained that the van was plugged in due to the extreme cold weather to prevent the oil and engine from freezing up.

"What did I get myself into?" was my thought, and it was only day one. After getting in the van, my most important stop was at a store to get winter gear. My face, hands, and feet were burning from the cold. The 1998 Olympic bobsleigh events began in Canada Olympic Park, just outside of Calgary. I had to wait until the athletes finished training, before taking them back to the hotel. I walked up the track, sporting my new winter gear, so bundled up that the movement I made was difficult, but at least I felt warmer than an hour earlier. My eyes were the only exposed part of my body. If I could have found my way around without looking, those too would have been covered. I found a spot that was flat, it was a platform built up that overlooked part of the track. From this vantage point, I could see one curve to my left, then a straightaway that ran into a loop. I was amazed at how narrow the straightaway was, and how tall the curves were, all were covered in ice.

I stood next to a guy, who introduced himself as the

coach for the Canadian team. I told him who I was and what I was doing here. Of course, my conversation to him took a few tries, as I was adamant to not remove any coverings on my face in case it froze. It was probably not polite to try and speak with a mask covering your mouth. As the bobsleighs came down the track, I was amazed at the speed. I stood about 3 feet from the track, and I could almost reach out to them. The bobsleigh rode vertically up on the curves. After about 15 bobs had descended, I got brave and removed my mask so I could ask questions. This sport had gotten me intrigued. The coach gave me a brief explanation, what the bobs do, or don't do, and the aim for the pilot in the curves.

I kept asking questions, even though my hands, feet and face were numb. Four hours had passed and I was even more intrigued by what I saw. I waited at the bottom of the track, ready to pick the guys up. At the University of Idaho, one of the original team members of the Jamaican bobsleigh team competed in athletics. In my volunteering with the men's program, I had gotten to know him really well; Chris Stokes was the one that invited me to Calgary, that's how I got my start in the sport of bobsleigh. I was able to get a chance to go down the track as a brakeman. After a harrowing, frightful experience of speed and G-forces, with my head tucked between my knees. I decided that being in the back was not for me. I wanted to drive.

Calgary, Alberta, Canada 1992

I came back to a place that would become my "home track" for the next 15 years. It was time to attend the Federation International de Bobsleigh et Tobogganing (FIBT) pilot school. A year before I had seen the sport, and that's when I wanted to learn how to drive. Unlike most sports where one can learn in slow motion or rehearsal, bobsleigh is learned by doing; literally. The bob and crew are sent off onto the track, and the best will survive. A week of this changed my life forever.

Olympic Year 1993-1994

As a qualified bobsleigh pilot, I was ready, or so I thought, for my first competition. Training comprised two runs per day for three days, then two races of two heats each. On the very first run of training, I crashed in a curve numbered 4, sliding on my head to the bottom, ending at curve numbered 14. It was embarrassing and scary to think I couldn't make it down safely. Of course, my Jamaican friends were at the bottom to cheer and help me; as any true West Indian would have done. I was harshly chastised by the race committee for being unsafe.

Fortunately, the team captains gave me a chance; they allowed me to get extra training runs in later, from the ladies luge start. After an uneventful night, I was ready for the next day. I managed to race, and finish right-side up in my first ever bobsleigh competition. After the races, the Jamaicans mentioned that I was very close to points needed to qualify for the 1994 Olympics to be held in Lillehammer, Norway. Therefore, what I needed to do was to compete in three more races on two different tracks and gain a few more points, I think it was around 8-10 points.

My next stop was to Lake Placid, New York. I had another nightmare waiting for me. This track was quite different from Calgary, with larger curves, speed and difficulty. Keeping true to form, I crashed twice in training, but managed to stay upright in the races and gained qualifying points. As the season was ending, due to an Olympic year, my only other option was to race at Cortina D'Ampezzo, Italy. I had never been to Europe and had no idea where to go, stay, the track layout, and etc. I did get the information I needed and made my way to Italy.

Cortina's track was quite similar to Lake Placid, but also more difficult in areas. My confidence was shaky at best, after a disastrous crash in Calgary and Lake Placid, all I needed now was to complete a successful race here and I'll be qualified for the Olympic Games. Again, during the final training run, I crashed. Actually, I crashed twice. I crashed on one corner, with the bobsleigh on top of us. As it continued sliding down the track, it abruptly hit an exit, and unknown to me it flipped us right side up. My only concern at the time was to pull my head off the ice and get under the cowling. Unfortunately, this lack of judgment, caused the bobsleigh to crash again at the next curve; as no one was driving. After being berated in English, French, Italian and German for not being "qualified" to race here, I made my way back to the hotel. It was a restless, sleepless, and stressful night. I knew I had to get up and race the next morning, which I did. Successfully completing my two runs and qualifying for the 1994 Olympic Games.

I always believed in myself. I knew that I had what it took to be successful, but I needed to understand what I was doing, and not doing caused me to keep crashing. I saw others being successful, and felt they were no different than me. I had the mental toughness to make it; I just needed to figure out how. In the end, after many years I did learn to persevere, I did learn to manage stress; I did learn that if someone wants something badly enough they have to keep at it. Many will say you can't, but with resources and some luck, it can happen. I did manage to keep upright at the Lillehammer Olympics, and made it back for 1998 Nagano and 2002 Salt Lake City Olympics. A strong self-belief, commitment, and goals will get you to the places you only dreamed about.

Greg Sun literally crashed his way to the top. He knew that he was no different from other people. He knew that he too could learn how to drive a bobsled, as long as he was willing to pay the price, and learn the basics. Dad always tells us that everything is hard at the beginning. We just have to stay in the game long enough to learn the basic skills and then what used to be hard will get easier. Do what Greg did. Don't quit. Learn the basics. And realize your dream.

Duff Gibson
Skeleton - Canada
Salt Lake City 2002; Torino 2006

Duff Gibson is Canada's first Olympic gold medalist in skeleton and 39 years old at the time of his win. He currently holds the record for being the oldest individual gold medalist in Winter Olympic history. Gibson's family had been active in national and international competition for much of Gibson's life: his father was a Canadian lightweight judo champion and his uncle represented Canada in rowing at the 1984 Los Angeles Games. Duff currently coaches the Canadian skeleton team.

Use Your Strengths

My dream since I was 10 years old was to compete at the Olympics. My "ignition point" came when I watched the 76 Olympics in Montreal. There were many events that I saw at those Games that I still remember very clearly today, such as Nadia Comaneci's perfect 10s in gymnastics and Bruce Jenner's win in the decathlon. For whatever reason, those few weeks had an almost magical effect on me and I knew that I wanted to be a part of it and I honestly didn't remotely care what sport it would be in.

My biggest struggle I had to overcome was actually figuring out what was the best sport for me. I competed in wrestling, rowing, speed skating, bobsledding all at a national level, and even at an international level in bobsledding before I found my sport which is skeleton. Skeleton requires what I happen to be good at and doesn't penalize me for what I'm not so good at. It took a lot of time and perseverance to get there but what kept me going and in all honesty made it fun was the fact that I was doing something that I loved to do. I love to compete and trying to get better. I love the training in a sport. For the whole journey, I was just doing what I loved to do.

It didn't feel exactly how I thought it would when I made the Olympics and it didn't actually feel how I thought when I won the Olympics either. There was a great relief and a sense of satisfaction in achieving my lifelong goals but at the same time I was struck by how little my life changed. The things that were really important to me before were the same things as after. The cliché about life being a journey and not a destination, to me at least, it is true.

Duff knew he wanted to compete in the Olympics. The sport he picked did not matter to him. He just wanted to be an Olympian. He tried many different sports until he found a sport that fit him just right. A sport that used Duff's strengths. By finding the right sport, Duff not only became an Olympian, but he also became an Olympic Champion. Dad's strength was perseverance. He picked the luge because he knew there would be a lot of quitters and he would simply not quit. Find your strength and use it to realize your dream.

*"You have to train your mind
like you train your body."*

*- Bruce Jenner
1972, 1976 Decathlon*

Jonathan Edwards
Luge - USA
Lillehammer 1994

Jonathan Edwards competed in the doubles luge in the 1994 Lillehammer Olympics. Jonathan helped coach my dad for the 2010 Vancouver Olympics. He also helped fix up my dad's sled right before the 2002 Salt Lake City Olympics so that Dad could compete. Jonathan is a lot of fun. We love it when he visits us from his home in Canada. Jonathan is a world class lacrosse goalie coach and he owns a furniture store in Calgary.

The Power of Books

My Olympic dream started in 1988. I was invited to a luge camp in Lake Placid, NY to try luge on ice. I had tried luge on wheels in 1984 when I was ten and a half. And then again in 1987 when it was part of a nationwide recruitment camp. I was actually in Lake Placid staying at the old Olympic Training Center trying luge for the first time while the Olympics were going on in Calgary where I now live.

I wouldn't say that there was a point when the Olympic dream "clicked" in me. I do remember being left off the 1992 Olympic team and thinking "Never again will I let my Olympic dream be left up to a bunch of coaches." Even though we were left off I went over to Albertville to watch opening ceremonies and to watch all of the sliding competitions. I remember sitting in opening ceremonies and thinking, "This sure beats any college lacrosse game I'm ever going to be involved in." So, right about then, I decided that I wasn't going to pursue college lacrosse in favor of trying to go the 1994 games.

As for the biggest challenge I ever had to overcome in my Olympic dream: It actually came AFTER I had decided to retire from luge. You see no one had prepared me for what was going to happen after my dream was over. It's ok to have a dream but your dream shouldn't be the end of things, it really needs to be the beginning of many other dreams. So many of my classmates and people of influence in my life at that time had told me that there would never be anything like my Olympic experience. Nothing was going to compare. They would tell me things like, "It's all downhill from here." To be honest, that didn't make me feel so good.

Keep Pursuing New Dreams

This was really hard to deal with and I'd say it took me a good twelve or fifteen years to really realize that that wasn't true. It was a lot like realizing that the wake of the boat isn't what drives the boat. It's the engine that drives it. And as the captain of the boat you've got the ability to turn the wheel and make that engine go wherever you want that boat to go.

I now think of my life in those terms. The Olympics was one thing in a long list of things that I wish to accomplish in my life. People think that as an Olympian you are gifted with this amazing genetic code that wires you to do amazing things. I would disagree. Going to the Olympics is a lot of hard work, but it's a lot of fun too. I'd say, that on a day to day level, there are more single mom's working three jobs to raise their kids that work harder than what most Olympians do, it's just a different path. As Olympians our hard work takes us onto a stage that the whole World gets to see. But the recipe is the same.

Now that I am an Olympian I look forward to additional challenges in my life. Being an Olympian is not what defines me, it is a unique accomplishment that allows me to go forward and know that I can accomplish other great things. I now live in Calgary, a city that I fell in love with when I was 15. I have two great kids which day to day is harder to deal with than ANY Olympic training! And I own a great business which now allows me to do other great things with my life.

So how did I get through that challenge of what to do after my Olympic dream was accomplished? I read. I read a lot. I mean a whole lot. The nightstand next to my bed is a big fire hazard with all of the books and magazines and reports that I print off on the Internet. If we struggle at any point in our life, like I did after my sporting life was done, we only need a tidbit of information to help us through that point. And how do we get information? We read. And I never know when I'm going to read something that is going to change my life so I read. Or I listen to a book on my iPod. Either way I am always learning and when I started to do this I changed my life.

Now every day to me is filled with opportunity. For many people this just isn't the case. They feel that they have no options. That they can't do it. That the world is easy for others but not so easy to them. That's a load of horse you-know-what. When you read you start to hear the stories of others who have had the same struggles and what have overcome them. You have to always fill you brain with ideas to overcome any struggle. If you read you have ideas. If you have ideas you have solutions. If you have solutions you can overcome any challenge.

Maybe the reason my dad and Jonathan Edwards are such good friends is that they both love to read. Ever since I can remember, both my mom and dad have read to both my brother and I. Everyone in our family loves to read. Our house is full of bookcases. We even have baskets filled with books everywhere. Sometimes my parents have to tell us to stop reading while we're eating dinner. But it's fun! And you learn so many neat things from all the books. I like how Jonathan does not worry about life's challenges because he knows he can always find answers in books. Knowing that helps you be more confident every day.

"If you think you're done, you always have at least 40 percent more."

- Lauren Crandall
2012 Field Hockey

PART THREE

Commit to Your Dream

Scott Hamilton
Figure Skating - USA
Lake Placid 1980; Sarajevo 1984

Scott Hamilton was the US flag bearer at the 1980 Lake Placid Olympics. When my dad was 21 years old, he watched Scott Hamilton win the Gold medal at the 1984 Sarajevo Olympics. Watching Scott Hamilton inspired my dad to pursue his dream of becoming an Olympian. Today Scott Hamilton is a figure skating analyst and a professional speaker.

Do what Others are Unwilling to Do

When I started skating at age nine, I never thought that I would ever be good enough to even think about actually competing in the Olympics.

I started because there was a new rink in my home town and my parents were given the suggestion that they needed a day for themselves to recharge their parental batteries.

I was in and out of hospitals for years and my mom and dad were near the end of their strength to endure the responsibilities of their sick, adopted child.

Saturday mornings at the skating rink turned out to be that day.

My mother LOVED the fact that I started skating. She would parade me all over the neighborhood with each test passed or each medal won. She would say "He passed his test with flying colors!" Or "He won his competition by a landslide."

Even with the successes, I was an underachiever. But she was blind to that.

It wasn't until her passing in May of 1977 that I decided that I was determined to be everything that she thought I could be.

Ranked ninth in the world in 1977, there didn't seem to be any way that I could make up the ground needed to make the team in 1980.

Decide to Work Harder than Anyone Else

That didn't stop me. I carried my mother with me every step of every practice everyday. I learned new jumps, spinned faster and got through my entire routines each day preparing to be better than I have ever been.

I realized that I was the only reason I hadn't been successful in the past.

I also became aware that early in my skating career I didn't have the commitment and work ethic needed to defeat my competitors because they worked harder.

Now I was more determined than they were. More focused. More willing to do what they weren't.

In 1978 I placed third in the US National Championships and was named to the World Figure Skating Team.

The process of making it to the World Championships is the same as the Olympics, so that accomplishment allowed my first thoughts of becoming an Olympian.

After an injury that set me back in 1979, I was able to regain my third place ranking in 1980 and was named to the 1980 US Olympic Team.

To this day, I am convinced that every accomplishment I ever achieved in skating was due to the fact that I never slowed down in my training or gave up.

If you want to be an Olympian, you have to, at times, be lucky. You have to have the right physicality for the sport you are competing in. But most importantly, you have to do what your competitors are unwilling to do.

Work harder.

Work smarter.

Don't spend precious time doing things that will take you away from that opportunity.

But still have fun.

Love what you are doing and it won't seem like work.

Commitment. Repetition. Love of your sport. Respect

for your coaches.

Those all play a part in achieving any goal in sports.

But there is also a "trickle down effect" that comes with putting yourself in the right places.

Due to my unique story of sickness, personal loss and determination I was elected by the USA Olympic Athletes of the 1980 Olympics to be the flag bearer in the Opening Ceremonies.

It is still a memory that gives me goosebumps!

Four years later in Sarajevo, I won the Gold Medal.

During the Medal Ceremony and the playing of the United States National Anthem, I remember looking back and remembering all the people that made both Olympics possible and wonderful.

The most memorable being my mom.

My brother and I are judo players. We actually get to train at the Olympic Training Center in Colorado Springs under 1984 Los Angeles Bronze medalist Ed Liddie. Coach Ed teaches us that if we have fun and work hard, we will improve and we will do better in our competitions. My dad gets more excited about us working hard than he does about us winning medals. Around our house, it's all about hard work and perseverance.

Vince Poscente
Speed Skiing - Canada
Albertville 1992

Vince Poscente competed in speed skiing at the 1992 Albertville Olympics. He's a best selling author and a professional speaker.

Commit to Your Dream

The opening ceremonies were on TV. I was captivated. Wouldn't it be cool to be an Olympic athlete? Yet, at 14 years old, I did nothing to feed the internal Olympic flame.

At 16 I forgot about "being cool" as I was out of my seat at the opening ceremonies of the Commonwealth Games. I cheered at the top of my lungs, "I love this! I love this! I love this!" Yet, still I did nothing. My Olympic dream fizzled because I lacked the one thing necessary to get to the Olympics or any worthy goal – commitment.

At 21 I joined the Canadian National Wrestling Team as their videographer for the Commonwealth Games in Brisbane. Everyone thought I was one of the wrestlers. Enjoying the notoriety I didn't correct anyone. Leaving Australia the customs official's eyes lit up as he saw the Games visa in my passport.

"Were you in the Commonwealth Games?" he asked.

"Yes," I said while that little voice inside said, Don't go there.

"What sport were you in mate?" he said leaning forward with a big smile.

"Wrestling," said knowing I was backing my integrity into a corner.

"Did you win?" he asked.

I replied with a meek, "No."

"Well how'd you do?" he said with unwitting, sympathetic eyes.

I searched for what to say, paused and said, "Fourth."

Then he did something customs officials never do. He came out from behind the booth, put both his hands on my shoulders and said, "Mate. Fourth is okay. I'm proud of you and I don't even know you." He made sure I was taking in every word. "Your country is proud of you. And... your parents are proud of you."

I never got busted in that lie but I did make a decision. Never would I say I did something that I didn't earn.

At 22 I competed in luge, but I quit when the national coach said I wasn't any good. Four years later, with a ticket for the Calgary's Opening Ceremonies I realized I made the biggest mistake of my life. Friends I raced with were marching in the Olympic Games and I was in the stands with a ticket.

My biggest struggle to get to the Games was not in between ages 26 to 30 in the sport of speed skiing. It was from age 14 to 26 when I didn't commit.

When I walked with the Canadian Olympic team in Albertville in 1992 I realized a dream that I ignored because of fear and ignorance. Fear of failure! Ignorance that commitment is THE most important step towards any dream.

Dad says that commitment is making a promise to yourself that you will do whatever it takes for however long it takes to make your dream a reality. It's not making excuses. It's focusing and doing what you need to do even when you don't feel like it. When I was trying to convince my parents that I was responsible enough to have a puppy I was committed. I was 100% focused for two years. And it worked! I got my puppy. Commit to your dream and don't make excuses. Commitment works!

"You can map out a fight plan or a life plan, but when the action starts, it may not go the way you planned, and you're down to your reflexes - which means your training. That's where your roadwork shows. If you cheated on that in the dark of the morning - well, you're getting found out now, under the bright lights."

- Joe Frazier
1968 Boxing

Eddie Liddie
Judo - USA
Los Angeles 1984

Eddie Liddie coaches my brother, Gracen and I in Judo at the Olympic Training Center in Colorado Springs. He is a very special coach because he cares so much about how we do. Judo is a very challenging sport but Coach makes it fun. I feel blessed to have such a terrific coach. Coach Liddie serves as the High Performance Director of USA Judo. He creates programs that help athletes make the Olympic team; the vehicles for the athletes and coaches to be the very best that they can be.

Stay the Course

Both of my parents were black belts in Judo. My dad was a New York City police officer and he owned a store. After school, Dad coached the neighborhood kids in Judo to teach them discipline and life values.

I started Judo like anyone else just doing it as a junior; the only difference was that my dad was my first coach. I quit Judo in high school to do the popular high school sports like basketball, etc. My dad talked me into returning to Judo by asking me to help coach the kid's class. He enticed me by offering to raise my allowance and it worked.

I competed off and on and was very lucky to run into the Cumberland College Judo Team at a tournament. They offered me a half scholarship to attend their college and be a part of their team. Just like a lot of young kids I watched the Olympics and dreamed at times of participating in them. But it was my freshman year in college when I realized how badly I wanted it and that I really could make the team and pursue winning a medal. After competing in my first World Championship I understood how big the challenge would be.

My biggest challenges on the way to the Olympics were money, knowledge of the sport, and guides. I thought I knew the sport but after participation in my first world championship in Paris, I understood that I had a lot of work to do but I could get it done if I stayed the course. Staying the course is so important. Many people have the talent, but only few have the will and desire to do what it takes.

Competing in the Olympics and winning a Bronze medal was the ultimate feeling. It was a combination of a sense of relief and incredible satisfaction. I often describe it like I died and went to heaven. The last 30 seconds of the match seemed like it was in slow motion, until the buzzer sounded. It was great getting to share the experience with my family who had been very supportive throughout the entire journey. It was not always easy or clear cut but it was always the target for all.

Coach Eddie started in Judo as a junior and quit in High School to play other sports. Eddie's dad talked him into returning and ended up getting a college scholarship. This lead into competing in the World Championships and eventually in the Olympics. The key to Eddie's success was staying the course. Staying in judo long enough to learn the skills and the techniques that result in success. Today Coach Eddie is passing on judo's life lessons to the next generation.

Eileen Coparropa
Swimming - Panama
Atlanta 1996; Sydney 2000; Athens 2004

Eileen Coparropa is a freestyle swimmer from Panama. She who won a silver and a bronze medal in the women's 50m freestyle event at the Pan American Games. Eileen's nickname is "La Sirena de Oro," which means the Golden Mermaid. Elleen graduated from Auburn University and is a supply chain strategy manager at T-Mobile.

Focus on the Dream

I competed in swimming in the 50 and 100 meters freestyle in Atlanta 1996, Sydney 2000 and Athens 2004. I was only 15 when I went to my first Olympics and I was honored to be the flag bearer in all three Olympics during the opening ceremonies.

I had many struggles during my Olympic cycles but I have to say the two biggest ones for me were being away from my family and fighting for strength after discovering I had an illness just two months before the 2000 Olympics. After the 1996 Olympics I finished high school in my home country and then moved away from my family to the United States to train and be able to make my team go to the 2000 Olympics. This meant I had to be away from my family and not being able to spend special dates such as holidays with them.

Being only 17 at the time, I really had to find inner strength to fight my feelings and really stay focused on what the goal was. Just two months before the 2000 Olympics I was very ill and had to quit training for about three weeks. During those three weeks I had to figure out how to do as much physical activity as possible and again, stay focused on my goal.

I feel that when you have a dream, it is sometimes hard to stay focused because of things that happen that are out of your control. I learned to stay focused and not let all those "outside" things keep me distracted; not giving up and always utilizing my family as my support team.

Looking back I realize I had several obstacles for both 1996 and 2000 Olympics. For the 2004 Olympic Games I knew this was my last chance to do something big for my country. I made the semi-finals in my event and I was the only woman in the history in my country to make it that far. It is an unbelievable and unexplainable feeling how good it feels when you can finally say, "I did it!" My goal was always to make my family and my entire country proud and I feel after the 2004 Olympics I could finally claim that I reached and surpassed my goal.

Eileen was away from her family while still very young and had to learn how to stay focused on her goal. Like Eileen says, sometimes it's hard to stay focused. Dad puts pictures of his goals and dreams all over his office to help him stay focused on his goal. Dad says the dream gives you energy and the courage to overcome the obstacles that will come your way so you have to surround yourself with your goal to stay energized. If you focus on your dream, the dream will give you the power to reach the goals on the way to your dream.

"I hated every minute of training, but I said. 'Don't quit. Suffer now and live the rest of your life as a champion."

- Muhammad Ali
1960 Boxing

Kristina Groves
Speedskating - Canada
Salt Lake City 2002; Torino 2006;
Vancouver 2010

Kristina Groves is one of Canada's most successful speedskaters. She won many World Cups and World Championships and four Olympic medals. Kristina majored in kinesiology and graduated from the University of Calgary. She's a professional speaker, a performance specialist, a CBS sports analyst, and an environmental advocate.

Stay in the Game

My first Olympic dream was sparked when the Olympics came to Calgary in 1988. At first I was captivated with the idea of running with the torch in the Olympic torch relay that would travel across Canada before the Olympics. I remember filling out a ballot at the Petro Canada gas station and dropping it in the box with the hopes that I would be chosen. I was so inspired by the torch run that I even went for a run down the dirt road at our cottage, holding a hammer up with my right arm pretending it was the Olympic torch. I was only eleven years old and I never did get chosen to run for that relay, but my Olympic curiosity was piqued and I was glued to the television during those Olympic Games.

It was then that I discovered the sport of speed skating, watching the legendary Canadian speed skater, Gaetan Boucher, skate his final Olympic race. He didn't win but something about his race inspired me and I wanted to try it too. I found a speed skating club in my hometown of Ottawa and have been doing it ever since. And can you believe it just before the Olympics in Vancouver I got to run with the Olympic torch, and that was a dream come true.

Improving was Always the Goal

I was not a very good speed skater when I was young. I was very skinny, weak, and slow. I did not win a lot of races those first few years but I was lucky for two reasons. For starters, there weren't many girls in speed skating at that time so I still felt encouraged by my results even though I was not very good, and I just fell in love with the sport. I had faith in my Olympic dream. From day one it was my dream to make it to the Olympics. Even though for many years, to many people, it perhaps seemed unlikely, I kept doing it because I loved it and enjoyed the challenge of improving.

I would say the biggest struggle I faced on the way to the Olympics was simply to find a way to get fast, even though it seemed that I was not good enough. The biggest challenge was to constantly learn and apply what I had learned from all my races and experiences to the next races. Improving was always the goal. It was a struggle because it took a really long time to get to the highest level. Once I started racing World Cups, it took me seven years before I stood on the podium with my first World Cup medal. I won my first World Cup medal when I was 27 years old and my first Olympic medal at age 29. I had to learn to be patient and work incredibly hard to get there, but of course in the end, the struggle is worth it.

Go from One Dream to Another

To make it to the Olympics, and then to win an Olympic medal was absolutely a wonderful experience. There are never any guarantees that you will succeed, even if you work incredibly hard, so to be able to fulfill a dream, especially within a tiny timeframe of one race on one day, is a remarkable feeling of accomplishment and joy at having achieved something that is truly so difficult to do. It is a very wonderful feeling, but I also quickly recognized that the feeling, although it stays with you forever in your heart, it is something you have to let go of if you want to continue to move forward, improve and grow.

I certainly enjoyed those moments standing on the podium, but I was always aware of the need to strive for

106

newer and greater challenges and not get stuck living in the past. I also remember being more thrilled with the feeling I had in those races, as opposed to the feeling of having won a medal. To hit that feeling on that one day you had a chance to do it, was for me, the greatest reward of all.

Kristina stayed in the game long enough to learn the basics and to improve. Her patience and attitude of constantly trying to improve paid off. Dad says that there is no such thing as an overnight success. You have to win many personal victories before you get to win a public victory. Stay in the game long enough to improve. Develop patience like Kristina and one day you will win your victory too.

"Fight. Anyone can do it when it feels good. When you're hurting, that's when it makes a difference, so you have to keep fighting."

- Erin Cafaro
2008 Rowing

PART FOUR

Take Action

Janet Evans
Swimming - USA
Seoul 1988; Barcelona 1992; Atlanta 1996

Janet Evans is considered the greatest female distance swimmer of all time. She competed in the 1988, 1992 and 1996 Olympics. Her record in the 400-meter freestyle stood for 18 years, her world record for the 1500 stood for 19 years and she still holds the world record in the 800. Janet is a spokesperson, an professional speaker and a TV personality.

Think Long Term

I first dreamed of the Olympics when I attended the 1984 Olympic Opening Ceremonies as a spectator. I decided right then and there that I was going to do everything I could possibly do to reach my dreams of swimming in the 1988 Olympics.

My biggest struggle in achieving my dream of becoming an Olympian was learning to put away instant gratification for future reward. For example, I had to get up every morning at 4:30 to go to swim practice. Sometimes I just wanted to go back to sleep rather than get out of my cozy bed to go swim six miles in a cold swimming pool. But I knew that sleeping in would only be instant gratification and that my ultimate dream - or future reward - would be swimming at the Olympics. So I would get out of bed every morning and head to the pool, where I'd work my hardest to get better and better.

When I finally reached my dream, it all felt very surreal. But it was amazing. When I swam at my first Olympic Games, I knew that the most important thing is to believe in yourself, work for your dreams, and overcome the hard days (like the mornings I was really tired!)...and you can become and do anything you set your mind to!

Dad tells a story about when he was training for the Olympics and somebody offered him a piece of chocolate cake. Dad would ask himself "Do I want the cake or do I want to go to the Olympics?" He says it was an easy choice because he wanted to go to the Olympics so badly. If you want to reach your dream, do what Janet Evans says. Put away instant gratification and focus on your future reward.

Eli Bremer
Modern Pentathlon - USA
Beijing 2008

Eli Bremer competed in the sport of modern pentathlon. The modern pentathlon is a sport created by the military many years ago. It is supposed to show what a soldier in the 1800s who was caught behind enemy lines might have had to do to deliver a message to his commander. It's a combination of equestrian, swimming, running, shooting and fencing. Eli is a graduate of the U.S. Air Force Academy with an MBA from the University of Colorado. Eli's an entrepreneur and business owner. He's been a sports commentator for NBC and he's a professional speaker.

114

Outwork Your Competition

When I was 4 years old, I took a flight from the Colorado Springs airport with my mom. When we got on the airplane, there was a guy sitting in our row who was wearing a warm-up suit. He was an Olympian who had just finished competing in the US Olympic Festival in shooting. That man took two hours on the flight to tell me about the Olympics and the importance of the Olympics. At the end of the flight, he gave me his Olympic Festival baseball cap. For the next two years, I wore the cap all the time and that started my dream of going to the Olympics.

The hardest thing I had to overcome was my own lack of talent. When I was young, I was the worst athlete you could imagine. I was the kind of kid you would pick last on the playground, not because the other kids were mean, but because I really didn't bring anything athletically to the table. I tried out for the local swim team three times before they finally selected me and they were a very bad team. After five years of swimming, my parents pulled me aside one day and suggested I quit and pursue playing the piano because I was doing so badly. Fortunately, they supported me in my decision to quit piano and swim more. A couple years later, it paid off and I started to become a good athlete. But it turned out to be a very good thing that I had to work harder that I couldn't get anything I wanted in sports. I learned that hard work can overcome a lack of talent. When I went into Pentathlon years later, it helped me that I was willing to work very hard for years with only small increases in my performance.

Walking into Opening Ceremonies at the Olympics was amazing. I was near the back, so I could see this massive stream of US athletes walking ahead. As the lead of athletes came close to the stadium, everyone started chanting "USA USA USA." It was so loud that it sounded like the stadium was going to come down around us. That was the moment when it felt real and it was awesome.

Eli overcame a lack of athletic talent by working hard for many years. He was patient and understood that any improvement in his performance was worth many hours of hard practice. By working hard and by having incredible patience, he was able to realize his Olympic dream. Celebrate every small progress and stay focused on your dream. Work as hard as you can for as long as you need to and you can realize your dream as well.

"I've always believed that if you put in the work, the results will come."

- Michael Jordan
1996 Basketball

Dain Blanton
Beach Volleyball - USA
Sydney 2000; Athens 2004

Dain Blanton competed in beach volleyball in the 2000 and 2004 Olympics. Today Dain is a sports broadcaster and beach volleyball commentator. He's also a professional speaker.

It's Worth the Work

I first saw the Olympics on the television as a little kid. Watching the Winter Olympics made me wish that one day I could be in the Olympics. I just was not sure in what sport. There are many paths that will lead to your dream. You just have to find the path that is right for you.

As a child, I played every sport I could - basketball, soccer, baseball, volleyball, etc. From the time I was 10, I would spend all summer playing beach volleyball with my brothers in Laguna Beach, where I was born.

In High School I narrowed my sports to just basketball and volleyball because of their similarities and because of my love for each sport. In both volleyball and basketball, height and jumping ability are very important. By the time I was about to graduate from High School, I had college scholarship offers in volleyball from schools such as USC, Stanford, UCLA and Pepperdine.

I chose Pepperdine because of the Coach, the academics, the location and Pepperdine's volleyball tradition. I attended Pepperdine and won a national Championship in 1992 and then graduated with a degree in Public Relations in 1994. I began playing beach volleyball professionally right after college but at the time Beach Volleyball was not an Olympic sport so at that point I thought I would never go to the Olympics. Later that year Beach Volleyball was voted as an Olympic sport so my dreams were once again a possibility.

I made a decision to pursue my dream. I set my sights on 2000 and trained all around the world and competed to qualify for the games.

There are several qualifying events on the way to the Olympics. The entire process was a struggle.

In August of 2000 in the last qualifying event before the games, my team had to finish in the top four to make the Olympic team. When my partner Eric Fonoimoana and I placed 3rd in that final event in Belgium we were on our way to Sydney, Australia for the 2000 Olympics.

As hard as it was to get to the Olympics, it was all worth it. My Olympic experience was incredible. As I took it all in at the Opening Ceremonies and in the Olympic Village I felt the pride that comes from representing your country in a world stage.

Defeating Brazil in the final was the highlight of my career. All the hard work. All the days of playing when you didn't want to or didn't feel well. All the discipline. All the training. It was all worth it when we stood on top of the podium and they put those gold medals around our necks. We were on top of the World.

There are many ways to reach a goal, but you have to work hard with lots of focus to get there. Dain had to choose between basketball and beach volleyball. He made his choice, trained all over the world, and was able to win the Gold Medal. As he says, "it was worth the hard work."

Simon Arkell
Pole Vault - Australia
Barcelona 1992; Atlanta 1996

Simon Arkell competed in the pole vault for Australia. Simon was Australian and Commonwealth Champion and record holder in the pole vault. Today he lives in California. He is the founder and CEO of Predixion software. When we started collecting stories for this book, Simon helped us out by connecting us with many Summer Olympic athletes he knew.

Associate with Winners

When I was 11 years old, my step-father took me to see a movie about the 1976 Olympics. The movie portrayed some inspiring performances and my Olympic dream was born.

The problem was that I wasn't very good at sports, definitely not promising enough to make it that far. However, I had an incredible desire to make it to the Olympics and everything I did from that day forward involved someday competing in the Olympic games.

I grew up in Australia and fell in love with the sport of pole vaulting. Although I was not very good, I knew that pole vaulting was the sport I wanted to do. Unfortunately, the best pole vaulter in Australia was not good enough to qualify for the Olympics.

Learn From the Best

I decided to go where the best pole vaulters lived - USA. I applied for a college scholarship in the USA so I could learn how to become better. The plan worked. I went from being a reasonable Australian vaulter to one of the best in the World. I became the Australian and Commonwealth record holder and champion, and when I was finally selected to represent my country at the Olympic Games, I became the first Australian pole vaulter in 16 years to do so. I competed in 1992 and 1996 and had a career that no one except I could have imagined back when I was 11 years old.

My biggest obstacle was being Australian at a time when the country was not producing world class athletes in my event. I knew in my heart that I had to figure out a way to move to the USA but didn't know where to start. The breakthrough came when I competed in the US on a tour with the Australian Junior team in 1985. I saw firsthand how high the standard was over here (I live in California to this day) and even better, I was given access to a list of the universities in the US that offered track and field scholarships. I wrote to 37 of them and received only a few replies. I was offered a tuition and books only scholarship at 2 of the 37, took one, then moved over here, hoping that I could make my dream come true. When I got to the US I did everything in my power to train and compete as hard as I could and it worked. I improved from 16'9" to 18'5" in 5 short years, broke all the records from Australia and my US college, and made the Australian Olympic Team. It was a dream come true but one of the hardest challenges to overcome.

Getting to compete in the Olympics was bliss. I was living my dream by competing at the highest levels against people who had been my heroes, I was traveling around the World, getting recognition as one of the best, and I still look back at my career with so much pride for having overcome what no one else could ever imagine I had to overcome.

Simon knew that if he wanted to reach world class level in the pole vault, he needed to go to the US, where the top coaches were. It's like Dad always says, "If you have to cross a minefield, find someone who has already crossed it and follow them. Find someone who has done what you want to do." When dad decided he wanted to compete in the luge, he lived in hot and humid Houston. What did dad do? He went to Lake Placid, NY and learned how to luge from the best of the best.

When dad started speaking professionally back in 2002, the first thing dad did was to find an experienced and

124

successful speaker to mentor him. Dad drives my brother and I 45 minutes each way twice a week so that we can learn Judo from the National Coach. Dad says it's worth the drive so that we can be around greatness. Do whatever you can to learn from the best and you will reach your goals and dreams that much faster.

Barbra Higgins
Fencing - Panama
Sarajevo 1984

Barbra Higgins competed in Fencing at the 1984 Los Angeles Summer Olympics. She has a law degree from the University of Miami and Bachelors in Business Administration and Accounting from Florida International University. Barbara is the President of Asta, a company that helps small businesses with their accounting and fiscal processes. Barbara lives in San Francisco.

Do Whatever it Takes

I had always been very competitive, as long as I can remember, I was driven to be the best at everything I did. In my athletic life and specifically as a fencer, the Olympics were the natural goal. I began to believe it was possible when several friends who had competed in the Olympics in fencing said I was good enough to make an Olympic team, which was 5 years before I got to compete.

The biggest struggle I had was having to work and train at the same time. I was at my strongest in 1980, I trained while in college, but Panama joined the USA in their boycott of the Moscow games. I had to regroup and since I was out of college by then and just finishing law school in 1983, I did not have the luxury of earlier years of training at the University for free. I not only had to pay for all of my living expenses and also for my training and travel which was important for tournaments, so I got a full time job.

My schedule for the year leading up to the games was to wake at 5:30 am to run or weight train from 6:00 am to 7:30 am and then take a train to work from 9:00 am to 5:00 pm. Next take trains to my fencing salle 1 hour away, grab a bite to eat on the train and take lessons and practice from 6:30pm to 9:00 pm. Then drive home with a friend and get to bed by 10:00 to 10:30 pm and start again the next day. The weekends were filled with traveling to tournaments and to other salle's to practice.

You have to have a passion for your sport and the attitude that failure is not an option and of course tenacity and a strong support group. This attitude has helped me tremendously in my business life. To never give up and get the job done no matter what! My coach would say there are no excuses for winners.

Making the Olympic Team in 1984 was an extraordinary experience and has impacted my life in ways I would never have imagined. Not a day goes by that my experiences I had prior to, during and after the Olympics have not helped me achieve my goals.

Barbra focused on her Olympic dream and for years followed a grueling schedule to realize her dream. She worked out in the morning, worked a full day 9-5. Then fenced until it was time to go to bed. Then did it over again every day. On weekends she traveled to tournaments. Dad tells us that if you are willing to do whatever it takes for as long as it takes, success is just a matter of time.

"The only way you are going to get anywhere in life is to work hard at it. Whether you're a musician, a writer, an athlete or a businessman, there's no getting around it. If you do, you'll win. If you don't, you won't."

- Bruce Jenner
1976 Decathlon

David Kimes
Shooting - USA
Moscow 1980

David Kimes won back-to-back World Championships in shooting and was part of the 1980 US Olympic Team. Today he's a shooting coach and a great mentor to many successful young shooters.

No Deposit, No Return

On November 20th 1963, I was working at my first job after graduating from college. That day I heard the terrible news - President Kennedy had been assassinated. When I got home from work that day, I saw that I had received a letter from the U.S. Government. The letter said, "Greetings from the President. You are drafted into military service."

Since I was a two-time All American in collegiate rifle shooting, I wrote the US Army Marksmanship Unit requesting a tryout. Fortunately it was granted. The year of the 1964 Olympics I competed in my first tryouts.

Fast forward 35 years - 2009. I had been speaking for Hollywood High School Jr. ROTC classes for three years. A good friend had been diagnosed with cancer in his right shoulder. My friend asked me to teach him to shoot pistol with his other arm after his surgery.

I remembered Karoly Takacs, a world level rapid-fire pistol shooter from Hungary who had lost part of his right arm when a hand grenade went off prematurely during a military exercise. Rather than quitting on his Olympic dream, Karoly learned how to shoot with his left arm, worked extremely hard and won two Olympic competitions with world & Olympic records.

I set out to find Karoly's story. I found it on Ruben Gonzalez's web site! This led me to Ruben's video of his presentation highlights. That video made me look back at my career in a completely different way. I then showed Ruben's video, "Becoming Unstoppable" to my students.

After class one of the students told the teacher that he had been cut from the football team the previous fall and had decided to quit, but after watching Ruben's video he had decided to go out for football again.

I have many Olympic pins. My favorite one is a pin I got from John Naber, the 1976 Olympic Team swimmer. The pin is simple. Inside an Olympic wreath are four words: NO DEPOSIT, NO RETURN. Those words apply to almost everything you do in life. If you do not put good effort into what you are doing, you will not get much back. John Naber's pin reminds me of Winston Churchill's quote, "NEVER, NEVER, NEVER GIVE UP!"

Back to my story. My biggest struggle on the way to making the Olympic Team was having limited time to train because I had a full-time job. I trained before and after work every day and on weekends. Focusing on what I needed to do technically, physically and mentally to improve my shooting was very tough to do with a full-time job. Two years before the 1980 Olympic tryouts I decided to quit my job so I could train full time. For two years I lived off of my savings and from the US Army Reserve.

The added training paid off. I was able to win two World Championships with World Records. Winning those championships filled me with satisfaction. That feeling of accomplishment has become ingrained in my soul and has given me more confidence and focus and success in all my endeavors. All the effort had paid off. Remember, no deposit, no return.

I went on to qualify for the 1980 Moscow Olympics. Unfortunately, President Carter forced a U.S. boycott of that Olympics in Moscow. But, I like to say, "There is always something good about something bad. You just have to find it."

At the gathering of that Olympic team in Washington, D.C., I talked to many coaches and athletes. I learned their mental thoughts and training and coaching methods. The things I learned from them helped me improve in my sport and later in coaching.

Our Olympic shooting team went to Beijing China that

132

summer. My score there equaled the gold medal score in Moscow at the Olympics. No deposit, no return.

David was willing to pay a big price to realize his dream. His favorite saying, "No Deposit, No Return," is just like what my Dad likes to say, "You have to sow if you want to reap." In life, the "prize" comes only after you pay the "price." Don't worry about the price you will have to pay. Just focus on your dream and do whatever you need to do to reach it. The Prize will be worth the price.

"Falling in life is inevitable - staying down is optional."

- Carrie Johnson
2004, 2008, 2012 Kayak

PART FIVE

Don't Quit

Shannon Miller
Gymnastics - USA
Barcelona 1992; Atlanta 1996

Shannon Miller is the most decorated gymnast in U.S. History, and considered one of the greatest gymnasts the United States has ever produced. Shannon is the president of Shannon Miller Lifestyle and President of the Shannon Miller Foundation, dedicated to fighting childhood obesity. She's also a TV broadcaster and the author of several fitness books.

Don't Listen to the Naysayers

Many gymnasts seem to have the Olympic Dream in mind long before they step into their first competition. Growing up I had never watched gymnastics on TV and could rarely sit still long enough to watch the Olympic Games. I knew that I wanted to be a gymnast because that's what my older sister, Tessa, was doing. All I ever wanted was to be just like my big sis.

It was 1991, eight years after I had started the sport that I finally set my sights on earning an Olympic medal. I still remember that moment. I was competing in Catania, Italy. It was one of the best performances of my career. I ended the night by winning the All Around competition.

I marched out onto the floor, up onto the first place podium. They handed me my bouquet of flowers and put the gold medal around my neck. The arena, filled with thousands of people, suddenly became quiet. The music started. There I was standing on the first place podium, gold medal around my neck. I was wearing my red, white and blue uniform with U-S-A across the back listening to the sounds of *my* National Anthem; watching the American Flag being raised! At that moment I knew that this was all I ever wanted to do. I wanted to represent my country and I wanted to do it on the biggest stage possible. For a gymnast, that is the Olympic Games!

Don't Let Other People Limit You

There were many struggles on the road to the Olympics; injury, "burn-out," changes in my size and shape and the pressure I put on myself to be perfect at all times. However, the biggest challenge was to combat the idea of limits. People will always find a reason why you cannot succeed. You are too tall or too short, too big or too small. In 1992, in many people's perspective I was too young. I was only 15 years old at those Games. By 1996, at my second Olympics and 19 years of age, I was too old! I learned that no matter what you do in life, people will look for a reason for you not to succeed. We also fight our own personal doubts about what we can accomplish. I learned early that my job was to constantly find reasons why I *would* succeed.

The moment when an Olympic gold medal is placed around your neck is one of the most incredible feelings in the world. I felt a mix of joy, excitement, relief and even a bit of sorrow that it was now over. The gold medal is wonderful but it's just a symbol of that one moment in time when everything came together; the hard work and sacrifice. The hours of training, working through injuries and constantly seeking perfection in every move. When you finally reach that podium its absolute insanity!

Ever since I can remember, Dad has told my brother and I that if we want something badly enough and are willing to work hard enough, we can reach our dreams. He also tells us to surround ourselves with positive people and stay away from negative people.

Everyone thought Shannon Miller was too young to compete in her first Olympics and too old to compete in her second Olympics. If Shannon had listened to everyone else she would not have ever competed in the Olympic games. But Shannon only listened to her inner voice and the became the greatest US gymnast ever. Think about that.

Dad got started in the sport of luge when he was 21 years old. Everyone thought he was crazy. But he only listened to his heart and showed everyone they were wrong. Follow your heart and make your life an adventure.

Greg Louganis
Diving - USA
Montreal 1976; Los Angeles 1984;
Seoul 1988

Greg Louganis began competing in diving at age 9. By 16, he had won his first Olympic medal, a silver medal on the platform in 1976. At 24, he became the first man in 56 years to win two Gold Medals in diving by winning both the platform and springboard events. In 1988, competing against divers half his age, he became the first to win double Gold Medals for diving in two consecutive Olympics. Today, Greg Louganis is a diving coach in California.

Accept Life's Challenges

My first Olympics were at age 16 in 1976 at Montreal Games. I was so young I didn't feel I belonged there and just didn't want to embarrass myself or my family, I did win the Silver Medal on Men's Platform. Then four years later I made the Olympic Team again but was stopped by a boycott of the 1980 Olympic Games, President Jimmy Carter forbid us to compete in those Games. In 1984, I qualified for my third Olympic Team in Los Angeles and won two Gold Medals, Men's Springboard and Platform Diving.

1988 was my forth Olympic Team and in the Prelims of the Men's Springboard I hit my head on the board. That along with having been diagnosed HIV Positive six months prior was a major set back to my goal of being the first man to win two Olympic Gold Medals in two consecutive Olympic Games. After I hit my head in that split second I went from "Favorite" to win to "Underdog" and I had to focus one dive at a time.

Ryan White, the young boy who was a hemophiliac and contracted HIV thru his clotting factor, was my inspiration to fight thru to the end and not give up. I was successful in winning both events, and making history, and years later I did present my Olympic Gold Medal to Jeannie White, Ryan's Mom when I went public about my HIV status. I would say success is dealing with whatever is thrown your way because God doesn't give you more than you can handle.

Dad always says that life is tough so we'd better be tougher. Life will knock you down but winners always lift themselves up, dust themselves off, and get back to work

141

chasing their dreams. Greg Louganis has had some tough challenges. But he never quit. When you are going through challenges, stay strong.

Peter Vidmar
Gymnastics - USA
Los Angeles 1984

Peter Vidmar is the highest scoring American gymnast in Olympic history. Peter has worked for many years as the gymnastics commentator for CBS Sports and ESPN and continues to work as a journalist or broadcaster at each summer Olympics. He's also an author and professional speaker.

Learn from Your Failures

I started gymnastics at the age of eleven when my father read an advertisement in a local paper entitled, "Future Olympic Champions Sought in Gymnastics." I answered the ad. It was in a small junior high school gymnasium that I met Makoto Sakamoto, who had just retired from competing for the United States in the 1972 Olympics in Munich. I stayed with "Mr. Mako" for 12 years as he guided me to a number of national and international titles, World Championships, and 3 Olympic medals. He filled my mind with visions of what an Olympic experience could be like, he taught me how to dream, and he taught me how to work….to work very, very hard.

One of my biggest struggles came in Budapest, Hungary at the World Gymnastics Championships, just 8 months before the Olympic Games. I had qualified for the finals on the Horizontal Bar, sitting comfortably in 2nd place, and in a good position to become the World Horizontal Bar Champion.

There was one slight problem. I was suddenly having difficulty with a particular skill in my high bar routine—a tricky maneuver that I'd managed to pull off without a hitch in the preliminaries, but now was giving me problems. Indeed, this was the skill I needed to do if I wanted to win the gold medal. Even though I struggled with it in the warm up gym, I determined that I needed to include that skill and chose to go for it.

The gymnast who was in first place competed before me, and he made a big mistake. All I had to do now was perform my routine successfully, and I would become the World Horizontal Bar Champion.

145

I began my routine on track, feeling great. But then the time came to perform my big skill, a skill which involved letting go of the bar, performing a front flip and then catching the bar. Everything was on track except for one minor detail.......I didn't catch the bar. I missed it and fell 10 feet to my stomach. My chance at victory was gone in a fraction of a second. I choked.

I was crushed. Deep down I wondered if I would ever be able to rise to the occasion under pressure. Did I have what it takes? When the heat was on and it came time to do that risky skill, or one just like it, would I always crack?

Head down, that's what consumed my thoughts as I walked through the streets of Budapest. It wasn't until I got to the hotel and was halfway through the front door that my coach Mako caught up to me. I didn't much feel like talking to him but we were in the space between the hotel's double entry doors, the area that keeps the heat from getting out and, in this case, was keeping me from getting in. He had me cornered.

He said a lot of things. But this is what I remember: "This is not the end."

"Everything is a learning experience," said Mako, "even competition. What you did tonight can be a valuable learning experience. You can benefit from this."

That hit a nerve with me. He was right. This was a valuable learning experience. I didn't want to hear that but I knew he was right. That fall taught me something that I somehow hadn't completely learned until that night: Never—Ever!— take anything for granted.

I promised myself that from that day forward, if I was going to take risks, I was going to be ready for them.

For the next eight months, there wasn't a workout between Budapest and the Los Angeles Olympics that didn't include an extra session, or two, working on that high bar release. I worked on it and I worked on it, and then I worked on it some more. To be honest, I never really liked doing it because I frequently crashed. But I did it anyway. Always with the memory of a missed world title.

By the time the Olympics came around, that release and I were a lot more comfortable. Not quite eight months after the fall in Budapest I jumped up and grabbed the bar in the all-around finals at the Olympic Games. About a minute later I came back down—when I was supposed to. I scored a perfect 10 on the high bar.

What stands out most to me after that performance and after winning gold medals at the Olympics, was the overwhelming feelings I had of gratitude, especially after our team had won the team gold medal. As I stood on the victory stand with my teammates when we received our gold medal, my overwhelming emotion was of gratitude. I was grateful to all who helped me to accomplish this goal. My coach, my parents, my teammates, my wife, and God. You will go on to accomplish great things in your life. You will always go farther if you show gratitude to all who help you.

Peter Vidmar used his failures as a stepping stone towards his future success. When my dad competed in the luge, after every training session, the team would review videos of the day's luge runs and discuss how to be better the next day. When I'm practicing my piano and I make a mistake, my piano instructor shows me how to do it better next time. When practicing judo, it's the same thing. Coach constantly shows me how I can do a move better next time. Dad says that as long as you don't quit, there's always a next time. There's nothing to fear because there's always a next time. You never fail until you stop trying.

Laura Wilkinson
Diving - USA
Sydney 2000; Athens 2004; Beijing 2008

Laura Wilkinson took her first dive from the 10 meter platform was at the age of 15. After being told by one of her teachers that she was too old to start a new sport, Laura plunged into diving anyway. Nine months later, she was kicked off of her high school diving team for being a "waste of space." The next year, Laura won her first US National Title, made the US National Team, and earned a bronze medal at the World Cup. She went on to win several Olympic medals. Today Laura is a professional speaker.

Pay the Price

When I was about 7 years old, I watched some girls doing some gymnastics tricks in the playground. I saw what they were doing and figured I could do it too. The next thing I knew I was doing series of front handsprings down the sidewalk and my teachers were making comments. My mom put me in gymnastics shortly after.

I've always watched the Olympics on TV for as long as I can remember. Seeing Mary Lou Retton's perfect 10 finish to win Olympic gold became even more etched into my brain after I started gymnastics. At 8 years old I began dreaming of making the Olympics. I figured 1996 would be my best shot at making the Olympics because I would be 18, and I guessed it would be that long until I really had things figured out. I may have been only 8 making these plans, but they were very real and concrete plans in my head!

Around my 14th birthday, I was burned out on gymnastics. I was realistic, and as much as I loved the sport, I knew that I wasn't going to be Olympic caliber. But for whatever reason, that plan of making the Olympics wouldn't leave my mind and I just knew in my heart that there had to be something else out there that I was good at.

My 8th and 9th grade years I tried so many different sports - tennis, track, softball, drill team, etc., but nothing was the right fit. My mom ran into another mom of an ex-gymnast and she said her daughter had started diving and I should try it. So I did. From the very first moment on the pool deck, I knew this sport was for me. It was essentially gymnastics into the water. I knew right away that I was made for this. My Olympic dreams came roaring back into the forefront of my mind and in 2000, those dreams came true -

all of them!

I had many struggles from the time I started diving. My sophomore year of high school I had only been diving about 6 months and my high school diving coach kicked me off the team for being a "waste of space." Fortunately I was training most of the time with a really great club team after school, and that is where I began to thrive. It was tough being kicked off, but because of the support from my club team and coach, it just added fuel to my fire.

In 1996 (my original goal of making the Olympics) I missed qualifying for the Olympic Trials by less than 2 points on two separate occasions. I was devastated. After I missed my last shot at making it, I remember sitting on a bench just crushed and someone spotted me. 1992 Olympic gold medalist, Mark Lenzi, came and sat next to me. He said something along the lines of, "Laura, don't let this take you out of the game. Let it be more fuel for that fire that I know you have in you." I took those words to heart and began working even harder.

In 1999, I realized that in order to be serious about making the Olympic team I needed to train full time with no distractions, but I was on a full scholarship for diving to the University of Texas. I made the really difficult decision to leave my scholarship behind and return home to train the way I needed to with one hang up - I had no way to pay rent. My dad then helped me find an agent who got my first sponsor and that helped me pay rent to be close enough to the pool to train full time.

About 3 months before the 2000 Olympic Trials (which I had already qualified for), I shattered 3 bones in my right foot in a training accident at a meet in Florida. The way in which I broke it required surgery, but my doctor said that would keep me out of Trials. So we casted it the way it was and hoped that it would heal well enough to walk on, maybe jump off of.

I couldn't train normally but my coach had me stand up on the 10 meter platform on my one good foot and go through the motions of my dives. This was a tough time for me and many times I just wanted to give up. But my teammates, my coach and my family were all behind me, supporting me regardless of how crazy an attempt this now seemed. Ten weeks and 3 casts later, I got my chance to go to the Olympic Trials. I was very nervous and it was my first Trials, but I was so excited just to have my shot that I was nearly overwhelmed when I won by a large margin, placing myself directly on the Olympic Team.

I ended up winning Olympic gold in 2000, but in many ways making that team was just as tough a battle. My favorite moment from the whole journey was in Sydney standing on the 10 meter platform before my very last dive.

I had no idea what place I was in, but I knew I was in the hunt for a medal. Standing there waiting for my name to be announced for my final Olympic dive, it all just hit me - I was living out my Olympic dream in that moment. I was not only in the Olympic Games, I was in the Olympic final, in the hunt for a medal. I had dreamed and fought for that very moment for so long. At that point, it didn't even matter what the final result was, I was living out my dream. Getting to stand on top of the podium a few minutes later was just icing on the cake.

Laura faced challenges all along her diving career - first her coach kicked her out of the high school diving team, later, she broke her foot right before the Olympic trials. But she never gave up. Laura kept practicing and kept her focus on her dream - the Olympics. By being willing to pay the price, she made her dream a reality. Dad says that success is simple, but it's not easy. Laura's story proves it.

Nikki Stone
Skiing - Aerials - USA
Lillehammer 1994; Nagano 1998

In 1998, Nikki Stone became America's first-ever Olympic Champion in the sport of inverted aerial skiing. Nikki is a Magna Cum Laude graduate of Union College in New York. Today, she hosts group skiing adventures, sits on 7 different Olympic and Sports Committees, and travels the world inspiring audiences through her professional speaking.

Always Bounce Back

I dreamed of being an Olympian since I was five years old and saw Nadia Comaneci score a perfect "10" in gymnastics. I actually built my own Olympic podium out of tables and chairs because I wanted to see how it would feel to be an Olympic gold medalist. I pushed myself to my feet and threw my fists towards the ceiling in victory. A huge smile broke across my freckled-face as I imagined the crowds cheering around me and the camera bulbs going off left and right. I had my answer, it felt incredible!

That road of realizing my dreams wouldn't be an easy one though. In the season following my 1995 World Championship win, I was feeling pain in my lower back but wrote it off as a mere muscle spasm. I tried to press on through the soreness and pushed until I was in unbearable pain 30 feet off the snow upside down. Luckily, my body went into autopilot and I finished the jump but found myself at the bottom of the aerial hill unable to move two inches in any direction. I had learned that, throughout my years of continually launching myself 30 to 50 feet in the air, I had put stress on two of my discs and they had become badly misshapen, leaking fluids, and in serious risk of bursting. I kept visiting doctors in hopes that one would tell me I could return to my sport, but each doctor, ten in total told me that they felt this was the end of my career.

After trying every exercise and procedure possible with no improvements, I started to slip into a deep depression. With years of sports psychology training, lessons learned from endless setbacks, and a host of supportive friends, family, and coaches, it was a quote from General George S. Patton that finally put the grit back in my teeth. It was simple: "Success is how high you bounce when you hit rock bottom." I was ready to bounce back. It would require intense weight training and, in my current condition, it would be extremely painful, but no matter what I was bouncing back. A mere twelve months later, I entered my second Olympic Games and with a twisting triple-back-flip, I won America's first gold medal in the sport of aerial skiing. Upon seeing my name at the top of the Olympic scoreboard, I vacillated between giddy shrieks of laughter and outright sobs of tears. Not tears of sorrow, but tears of joy; because I was finally going to stand atop a real Olympic podium.

The full weight of this reality didn't actually hit me until I saw my country's flag slowly slide up the pole just beyond the sea of cheering fans. I thought back to that little pigtailed, freckle-faced girl who had made her own "Olympic podium" twenty-two years earlier. I realized that this moment represented the fruition of those dreams; this was what the hard work was for. This was what the pain was for. This was what the agony, the tears, the dedication and the endless sacrifices were all about.

Nikki hurt two disks in her back only two years before the Olympics. Rather than quit, she was inspired by George Patton's quote about bouncing back. Nikki decided she would bounce back no matter how much it hurt. That's the spirit of a winner. Someone who is willing to do whatever it takes to reach their goals. Dad is always quoting Patton to us. His favorite George Patton quote is, "If you're going through hell, keep going."

"My competition isn't resting!"

- Kim Rhode
1996, 2000, 2004, 2008, 2012 Shooting

Phil Mahre
Alpine Skiing - USA
Innsbruck 1976; Lake Placid 1980;
Sarajevo 1984

Phil Mahre grew up in a ski resort in Washington state. By the time he was 12, he and his twin brother Steve were such great skiers that ski companies were offering them sponsorship opportunities. Phil became a member of the US Ski Team when he was 15 and was competing in the 1976 Olympics just a few years later. Phil won the overall Ski World Cup title three times in a row from 1981-83 and went on to win the Gold in the Slalom at the 1984 Sarajevo Olympics. His brother Steve took the Silver medal. Today, the Mahre Twins run the Mahre Ski Training Center in Deer Valley, Utah.

Go From One Dream to Another

I was fortunate enough to be introduced to the sport of skiing at an early age. My father worked as a volunteer ski patrolman and then became the area manager of a small ski area — White Pass — in the state of Washington. When I was 9 years old, my family moved to the base of the mountain and this enabled me to ski every day after I returned home from school in the winter months. In 1968 as a ten year old I watched Jean Claude Killy of France win three gold medals at the Olympic Winter Games in Grenoble, France. It was the first Olympics I remember watching and everyone made such a big deal about it, that I thought it would be neat to go to an Olympics and represent my country. The dream had been born, as I looked ahead eight years to the 1976 Olympic Winter Games.

In the spring of 1973, I was named to the US Ski Team at the age of fifteen. Everything seemed to be on track to realize my Olympic dream. Unfortunately, things don't always go as planned. In November of 1973, just three days before I was to leave for Europe to start competing on the World Cup, while skiing at home, I was caught in an avalanche and broke my right leg. This was a small setback, as I would miss the 1974 season, yet it would become much larger as I would re-break my leg some nine months later, causing me to miss most of the 1975 season as well. After missing a season and a half of competition, I began competing again at our 1975 US National Championships, winning the Giant Slalom. My Olympic dream was back on track.

Now with just 11 months left before the 1976 Games, and having never competed at the International level, my chances of being named to the Olympic Team were still small. Never did I ever think I wouldn't make it there. I used the summer of 1975 to train and prepare for the upcoming season, training with my US Ski Team teammates. In December of 1975, just two and a half months before the Olympics, everything was falling into place, when I finished fifth in the first World Cup race of the season in Val D' Isere, France. Hard work, dedication, determination and perseverance had paid off. My Olympic dream became a reality two months later when the 1976 Olympic Alpine Ski Team was named.

Walking in the Opening Ceremonies with your teammates, and representing your country is such an honor. It brings many thoughts of your journey to get there to mind. All the time and effort put forth, friends, family, coaches come to mind. It's an emotional time that will be cherished forever. It's also a time when new dreams are born. Dreams of not just going to the Olympics, but possibly winning a medal. A bit like life, with each and every dream obtained, a new dream is born.

Phil Mahre says you should never stop dreaming. Dad says you should be thinking about your next dream as you are getting close to your present dream. It keeps you happy, focused, and it makes life that much more fun.

Derek Parra
Speedskating - USA
Salt Lake City 2002; Torino 2006

In 1984 Derek began roller skating and by 1996 he had become the most decorated athlete in the history of the sport. He had everything but an Olympic Medal. So in 1996, he switched from inlines to ice skates to chase after that medal. Just two years later he earned a spot on the 1998 US Olympic Team. In Salt Lake City 2002, after being selected to carry the World Trade Center flag into the opening ceremonies, the emotional evening inspired Derek through a remarkable 5000 meter performance on opening day of the Games. He briefly held the world record en route to a silver medal finish. That set the stage for a stunning world record finish and Olympic Gold Medal in the 1500 meter event. Derek is an author and a professional speaker.

160

The Dream is Worth the Wait

I first thought of being an Olympian when I was 14 years old. I was growing up in Southern California and was learning how to roller speed skate. Although roller speed skating was not an Olympic sport at the time, I was hoping that roller speed skating would become an Olympic sport in the time that it would theoretically take me to get to the top of that sport.

No matter what your dream is, you need to be prepared to fight for it and dedicate yourself to it knowing that the dream is worth the struggle.

All along the way from my early days on roller skates I struggled with financial support. I left home at 17 years of age to chase my dream. My parents emotionally supported my efforts but did not financially. There were times that I was forced to eat out of the trash cans to survive.

By the time I was 26 years old, I had won 18 world titles and set two world records in roller inline skating. I was the most decorated athlete in the history of the sport. I had won everything I could have won but had never had the opportunity to compete for and Olympic medal because my sport was not an Olympic sport.

Be Willing to Take Risks

At that point I made a huge decision in my life. I took a huge risk. I left the world of roller sports and made the switch to ice speedskating - a sport rich in Olympic history. I quickly set my goal of making the 1998 Olympic team. I

161

made the team but because of a clerical error was not able to start in Nagano, Japan.

I was devastated by not being able to race in Nagano, but made the commitment to train 4 more years to make the 2002 team and it was there that I won a Gold medal and set a world record in the men's 1500 meter long track speedskating event. I also won a silver in the 5000 meters.

Standing on the Olympic podium to receive the Gold medal in my home country was an amazing moment that I will never forget for the rest of my life and that I will try to share with as many children as I can. My journey to the Gold took me 18 years...it was worth the wait!

It took Derek 18 years to make his Olympic dream come true but as he says, It was worth the wait. If you dedicate your life to chasing your dream your life will be a great adventure.

"Nothing can substitute for just plain hard work."

- Andre Agassi
1996 Tennis

Devon Harris
Bobsled - Jamaica
Calgary 1988; Albertville 1992;
Nagano 1998

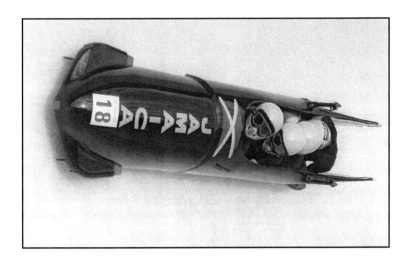

Have you ever seen the movie, "Cool Runnings?" It's the movie about the Jamaican Bobsledders. Devon Harris is a retired military officer and one of the founding members of the Jamaica Bobsled Team. He's the author of "Yes, I Can!" and "Keep on Pushing," the founder of the Keep On Pushing Foundation, and a professional speaker.

Focus on Your Goal

I started running track when I was 15 years old. At that time (1979), ABC Wide World of Sports was doing a series called "Road to Moscow". In it they featured athletes from around the world who were vying to compete in the 1980 Moscow Olympic Games. They not only highlighted the athletes' athletic lives but also their lives outside of the sporting arena. What I found inspiring about those stories was that Olympic athletes were average and ordinary people with extra-ordinary dreams. From that moment I too started to dream about competing in the Olympics

The most difficult challenge on the road to the Olympics was learning and mastering a brand new sport in a very short time and dealing with so many people telling us it couldn't be done.

We really kept focus on our goal of competing in the Olympics. We accepted that it was going to be difficult so we didn't allow setbacks and disappointments to discourage us. Whenever something went wrong, we evaluated the situation, made efforts to correct it and kept on going — focusing on achieving small successes every day. As for the naysayers, we used their words to motivate us. Every time someone told us it couldn't be done; it made us more determined to succeed.

Finally getting to the Olympics was amazing. Marching into a stadium filled with 60,000 screaming people and knowing that you can finally call yourself an Olympian is an unbelievable feeling. That one instant encapsulates what it is to be living your dream. Pride, a sense of accomplishment, gratitude that all the hard work has paid off as well as a sense of satisfaction that others have been inspired by your action.

165

Devon and the rest of the original Jamaican bobsledders had to fight for their Olympic dream when everyone was laughing at them and telling them their dream was impossible. Dad got to meet one of the Jamaican bobsledders at the Calgary Olympics. After noticing that some other bobsledders were laughing at the Jamaicans and being shocked at how they were treating the Jamaicans in a way contrary to what the Olympics are all about, Dad told the Jamaican, "I can't believe how they are treating you. How does it make you feel?" The Jamaican responded, "We're winners. We intend to get the last laugh." And they did. They kept bobsledding, they kept improving, and they became a very solid bobsledding team. They actually beat one of the US sleds at one of the Olympics. Because they kept fighting for their dream when everyone was laughing at them, eventually, they earned the respect of the whole world. Whenever someone laughs at your dream, that person should stop having any influence for you. Do what the Jamaican Bobsledders did. Focus on your dream, keep fighting, and you too will eventually earn everyone's respect.

"I've missed more than 9000 shots in my career. I've lost almost 300 games. 26 times I've been trusted to take the game winning shot and missed. I've failed over and over and over in my life. And that is why I succeed."

- Michael Jordan
1996 Basketball

Pernille Svarre
Modern Pentathlon - Denmark
Sydney 2000

Pernille Svarre competed in the modern pentathlon (swimming, running, equestrian, fencing, and shooting) at the 2000 Olympics. As a triathlete, Pernille has competed in the Ironman Triathlon. Today Pernille is both a personal coach and business coach and trainer.

Don't Give Up on Your Dream

My Olympic dream started in 1978 at the age of 17. I was tempted by my swimming coach to try out the Modern Pentathlon. My main and only goal was to qualify for the Olympics. Back then Modern Pentathlon for women was not an Olympic sport but I was told that it would become an Olympic sport in 1984. For the first three years I was training and studying business relations at the same time. I wanted to make sure I had something else to fall back on if I did not succeed in sports.

In order to reach my main goal I had to break time up into short-term goals to develop my skills. After finishing my studies in 1982, I was accepted by the US Modern Pentathlon Training Center at Fort Sam Houston, San Antonio to come train full time for five months. That's where I really learned about elite sports. Those five months of training were the best ever - five to eight hours of practice every day.

In 1982 we received some bad news. Women's Modern Pentathlon was not accepted for 1984 Olympic Games but maybe it would be in 1988. I kept training.

I went back to Texas every year from 1982 until 1996 to train. Every year I would train three to six months in Texas. It was my inspiration to continue fighting for my dream. San Antonio became my second home. During that time we got the same answer every four years, no room for Women's Modern Pentathlon at the Olympic Games. I still had an unfulfilled Olympic dream and I had no intention of quitting on it. I would not let myself down. I believed 100% that one day it would happen.

To kill time, challenge myself, and to make money I tried out the sport of Triathlon. I raced in the Hawaii Ironman

Triathlon in 1987 and 1988. Then I took 3rd place in the European Championship Olympic distance, 4th place at Europeans ½ Ironman and won the 1988 Nordic Cup Triathlon.

I also made the Danish national fencing Team and took part in two World Championships in fencing where I made the final 32.

At the age of 34 in 1996 I had to make a completely different decision. Becoming a mother was of course also a dream that I had. Because of my sport I had waited longer than most women but I decided that the time was right. I would have plenty of time to get back into shape after giving birth. My daughter, Frederikke was born in March 1997. Frederikke is my best gold medal ever, no comparison to the World Championship silver I won in 1984.

My mind was now split for a while but I continued keeping myself in shape in all five sports. I did not focus 100% on sport but I still focused enough to not miss any competitions. In January 1998, it was announced that Women's Modern Pentathlon would finally be an Olympic sport at the 2000 Sydney Olympics.

I made my game plan that day. I did a lot of quality training. I became stronger than ever and in 1998 I won the National Championships in cross country 8k running. I decided to peak at World Championships in 2000. This would be my last and only attempt to qualify for the 2000 Olympics. I had to place in the top 10 to qualify. My day was perfect it resulted in capturing the World Champion title. What a relief. Qualifying for the Olympic Games and winning the World Championship. The Olympics two months later did not go my way result-wise but I had reached my dream and I had completed my long journey.

Pernille's Olympic journey was incredibly long. She trained from 1978 until 2000 - 22 years, without knowing if her sport would even be included in the Olympics. Her faith and relentless work ethic is what makes Pernille a Champion. Don't give up on your dream. Fight as long as you have to. It will be worth it.

Bill Nieder
Shot Put - USA
Melbourne 1956; Rome 1960

    Bill Nieder won the silver medal in the shot put at the 1956 Olympics and won the gold medal in 1960 in Rome with an Olympic record throw. Nieder set the shot put world record on three occasions. He graduated from the University of Kansas and worked for 3M. He was instrumental in developing artificial athletic turf. Nieder sold the first-ever synthetic track surface for an Olympic Games to the organizers of the 1968 Mexico City Olympics.

172

Fight Till the End

When I was 20 years old I saw the movie depicting the life of Olympic champion Bob Mathias. At that time I was recovering from a severe knee injury I received in a football game between the University of Kansas, my school, and TCU. I had been in a full-body cast for four weeks and then a full-leg cast for an additional six weeks. I was told I would never play football again and possibly not be able to walk without an aid of some kind. I decided to concentrate on giving it a shot because I had experienced some success in track and field during high school. After watching the movie, the excitement, world travel, glory and the possibility of being the very best in the world on a given day sounded real good to a 20-year-old from a small town in Kansas. I immediately began to focus on achieving this goal.

My greatest struggle was my limited use of my right knee. I was blessed with the natural athletic ability, but the severity of the knee injury was going to be a very high hurdle to overcome. I immediately began a strenuous program to strengthen the knee and to improve my technique and upper body strength. Two years later I was on the US Olympic team, competed in Melbourne, Australia 1956 and won the silver medal but felt that I could continue my quest for the gold. Second place wasn't good enough. Two weeks prior to the Olympic trials in 1960 I stupidly went water-skiing and reinjured my knee. I was the favorite to take the gold in those games and ended up placing 4th in the trials, the first 3 make up the team. A really good friend and great track coach encouraged me to continue to compete and not give up he told me "you never know what might happen."

For the next two months I continued to compete and win

in track meets and in the last meet prior to the team leaving for Rome I set a new world's record. The US Olympic Committee called an emergency meeting and voted to send me as the 3rd team-member. I was called in the early hours of the morning and told to get to New York as I was now on the team. At the games I became the only alternate to ever win a gold medal on any US Olympic team. Winning the gold medal in 1960 was my greatest achievement. Words are not ever sufficient for me to describe my feelings as I stood on that podium. The pride I felt not only in myself but my country is really indescribable. The US had swept the event and we took a victory lap waving our flag to an absolute thunderous applause. These many years later I can still hear it and feel the excitement.

After breaking his knee, Doctors told Bill Nieder he would never walk without some kind of aid. Bill decided to follow his heart and started training for the shot put. Even after re-injuring his knee, Bill continued training, broke the World Record, and became Olympic Champion. When someone tells you that you can't do something, it's simply their opinion. If you believe in your heart that you can do it, ignore the naysayers, and chase your dream.

Daphne Jongejans
Diving - Netherlands
Los Angeles 1984; Seoul 1988;
Barcelona 1992

Daphne Jongejans is a Dutch diver who competed in three Summer Olympics. She is a graduate of the University of Miami and is in their sports hall of fame. Daphne is an event planner and the owner of Event Strategy Solutions. She lives in Atlanta, Georgia.

Face Your Fear

I started diving when I was 7 years old, shortly after the Olympic Games in Munich. My brother and I loved watching the diving on TV and made our parents wake us up and get us out of bed when the diving was on, so that we could see it. I don't think that the Olympic dream started then, although I thought going to the Olympics would be fun. Four years later I was already competing on the national team and saw that going to the Olympics could be possible if I worked hard. By the way, both my younger brother Edwin and I did make it to the Olympics.

Diving can be a scary sport. Whenever you learn a new dive it is not only frightening, but it can hurt. I had my share of wipe outs. I have never met anyone who was fearless. The biggest struggle I had was overcoming my fear to learn and perfect the harder dives that were required to make it into the top 12 in the world. That was the requirement that the Netherlands had for their athletes to qualify for the Olympic Games. The way I overcame my fear was to keep the end goal in mind and do a lot of positive self talk.

There was one other girl who was learning the same dives that I was and she was much braver than I was. Of course I couldn't let her get the better of me and decided that if she was doing those dives, I could too. Once I overcame the initial fear, it was a matter of discipline and practicing hard.

I know that many people thought I was giving up so much for my dream to be an Olympic diver, but I never saw it that way. Sure, I didn't get to go to many parties in high school, because I was either training or traveling, but I received so much more in return. I made friends from different nationalities and cultures, traveled all over the world and ended up going to college in the United States. I would have never had those opportunities without overcoming my fear and putting the effort into the training.

Competing in my first Olympics was probably the most exciting thing I have ever done. Walking into the Coliseum in Los Angeles for the Opening Ceremonies was nothing short of breathtaking. Actually having thousands of people watch the diving gave me so much energy that I set down my best performance ever. My favorite part was standing in line at the cafeteria right next to the athletes you have admired for years and always watched on TV.

Daphne had to overcome her fear of wiping out every time she learned a new dive. She used positive self talk (she gave herself a pep talk to help her take those scary dives). Facing her fear helped her overcome the fear. Then she practiced her new dive until she perfected it. Dad did the same thing with the luge. He was scared to take those luge runs. Sometimes he walked up and down the track for 20 minutes giving himself a pep talk. Finally, when the courage came, he took his runs. Surround yourself with people who believe in you. Give yourself pep talks. Tell yourself, "I can do it. I can do it. I can do it." Then face your fear like Daphne, and the fear will disappear.

*"The first thing is to love your sport.
Never do it to please someone else.
It has to be yours."*

*- Peggy Fleming
1968 Figure Skating*

Ben Hunt-Davis
Rowing - Great Britain
Barcelona 1992; Atlanta 1996; Sydney 2000

Ben Hunt-Davis won a gold medal in rowing at the 2000 Sydney Olympics, as a member of the British rowing team, the only British crew to have won this event since 1912. Hunt-Davis is a keynote speaker and owns Point8 Coaching, a corporate development company. He also works for the British Olympic Association.

Turn Defeat into Victory

I first remember watching the Olympics in 1980 when I was 8 years old. I remember my mother jumping up and down screaming at the TV as British athletes, Sebastian Coe and Daley Thompson won Olympic Gold Medals. It was incredible to watch them but I knew that I'd never be anything like them. I was hopeless at all sports. When I was 13 I started rowing and I was pretty hopeless at that too but over the next three years I started to improve. I loved racing and loved being on the water. I knew that I could never compete at the Olympics but I was sure that I could beat the people around me and I was sure I could do better that the boys in the year above me had done. By the age of 16 I had one goal in mind, to be a Junior World Rowing Champion, 18 months later I came 4th but the Olympics were now within reach.

During the nine years that I was competing I had a number of injuries and incidents that set me back but the biggest challenge that I had was losing. From the age of 18, until I was 28 I lost almost every race that I competed in. While I was at school I won a lot of regattas and loved racing, but from the Junior World Championships, where I was 4th, the Under 23 World Championships the following year, six world Championships, and three Olympic Games, I only won three races. They were the last three. For nearly a decade I lost every race that I took part in. I was surrounded by people who were winning and I kept losing, race after race after race. I was desperate to win, I was desperate to succeed but I kept losing and it was quite clear that most people believed that I could never win; most people thought that I didn't have what it took. Most people thought that I should give up my dream and find something else to do. I didn't listen to them. I just kept racing.

Everything came together in the Olympics. The Olympic final for the Men's Rowing 8 was an amazing race. We blasted off the start and got an early lead. We worked to extend it and then extend it again and again and again. We had given the first 1500m of the 2000m race every drop of energy we had knowing that we'd have the courage to see the last 500m through. I crossed the finish line not really knowing what had happened, I knew that we'd crossed the line first but I had no idea what it meant, I was too tired. But over the next seconds as I got more oxygen to my brain I realized that we'd done it. We'd won. We'd won the Olympic Gold Medal. We were Olympic Champions. Standing on the medal podium, I knew that every second of the last 10 years had been worthwhile. Despite all the setbacks, every defeat, every training session, every time I'd been told that I couldn't do it we'd done it. It was better that I ever dreamed it would be.

Ben was a good rower, but because of injury and other setbacks he was not able to win a single race in nine years. Most people thought he should just quit but something inside him, his desire to win kept him in the fight. When my brother or I are having challenges, when we don't see improvement in out performance — whether in piano or in judo — or whatever we may be working on, Dad reminds us to keep practicing and to stay in the game. Sometimes you are growing inside, and it may take a while for your outside results to catch up with your inside growth. When you are going through a slump, don't quit. Keep practicing the basics and before long you will get out of your slump.

Dominic Johnson
Pole Vaulting - St. Lucia
Atlanta 1996; Sydney 2000; Beijing 2008

Dominic Johnson competed in three Summer Olympics in the pole vault for St. Lucia. He's a graduate of the University of Arizona. He lives in Tucson, Arizona, where he manages his business "Isabella's Ice Cream." Johnson set up a College Athletic Scholarship program that helped over 30 St. Lucian athletes, one of who went on to become a 2004 Olympian.

Learn to Deal with Failure

I was born on the tiny island of St. Lucia in the Eastern Caribbean, and I therefore have dual citizenship. At age 15, I started Pole Vaulting, and by age 17 I had fallen in love with the sport and knew I was going to make it a career. It was at this point that I set my goals to become an Olympian. Just three years later I jumped for the first time over 18 feet, thus meeting the Olympic qualification standard.

Fortunately my parents we very supportive of my dreams, and I was very focused. The most important advice I can offer is to become a champion you must learn to accept and deal with failure. In sports and in life you do not win all the time, in fact, you are lucky to win half of the time. Every time I had a disappointing result I asked myself "what did I learn?" I found that I always learned more from my failures than from my success. I now carry this same philosophy into my non-sport life.

The year I first qualified for the Olympics was very exciting because that season I improved my personal best by nearly two feet, an amount almost unheard of. As a result of such a quick improvement my jumping was very inconsistent. When I walked into the Olympic Stadium in Atlanta I stared at the crowd and my legs quit working. Only four months before I was jumping at a high school level and now I was jumping with the best in the world, including my idol, at the time world record holder, Sergey Bubka. My nerves got the best of me and I failed to clear my opening height. As it turned out, Sergey Bubka also had the same results that day. Rather than dwelling on my result, I learned as much as I could. I took those lessons from that experience and become a better athlete as a result.

Dominic learned how to deal with failure. He understood that failure is temporary as long as you refuse to quit. He always looked for the lesson in every failure. Dad tells us that life is tough so we need to be tougher. That life will knock us down but we need to get right back up, dust ourselves off, learn from our struggle, and get back into the fight with our new knowledge - stronger and smarter than we were before. Learn from your mistakes.

Bruce Kennedy
Javelin - Rhodesia, USA
Munich 1972; Montreal 1976;
Moscow 1980

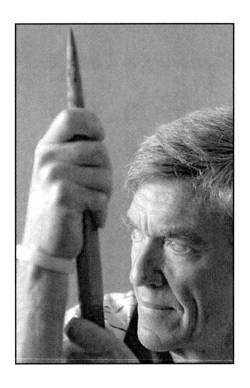

Bruce Kennedy is probably the best javelin thrower to never get to compete in the Olympics. He qualified for three Olympic teams, but politics kept him out all three times. His story is an amazing example of how to maintain a positive attitude in face of life's challenges. After graduating from Berkeley, Bruce got his MBA from Stanford, and is now co-founder of a successful investment partnership based in Camarillo, California.

The Fight Strengthens You

I grew up in a small African country, previously called Rhodesia and now called Zimbabwe. My father, a former middle distance runner, was very active in the administration of track and field in the country so from a young age I was surrounded by top athletes. I remember in 1960, when I was 9 years old, several track athletes were selected to represent Rhodesia in the Olympic Games in Rome, Italy. It was really exciting to know that our best athletes were going to be able to compete against others from all over the world. I remember listening to the news broadcasts on the radio. There was no television in the country at that time so I read in the newspaper about how all of Rhodesia's athletes were doing. The idea of following in their footsteps and representing our small country got me fired up and it became one of my athletic ambitions to one day compete in the Olympics.

The biggest struggle I faced, as an amateur athlete out of college, was finding ways to earn enough money while still being able to train. I graduated from the University of California Berkeley in 1973 and married my college sweetheart a few months later. I had been selected to represent Rhodesia in the 1972 Olympic Games in Munich, West Germany, but our team was disqualified because of political reasons. Although this was disappointing I was determined to follow my dream of competing in the Olympics so both my wife and I were willing to make sacrifices which would allow me to do that.

I was a javelin thrower and like many events it requires athletes to develop good technique to succeed. This can take a long time and a lot of patience plus one really needs to have a coach. I always believed that determination and discipline would pay off. In 1976, I was once again selected to represent Rhodesia, in the Montreal Olympics, but once again our team was excluded for political reasons.

Still determined, I continued to train without a coach and became a US citizen in 1977. That year I won my first US National title that year. Finally, my luck started to change. Through the US Olympic Committee I was able to get a job which gave me time to train. Late in 1979, Tom Tellez, who was at the University of Houston and also Carl Lewis' coach, started to coach me. In my first meet in 1980 I threw a lifetime best, it was my first improvement in just under seven years. I stopped and thought about that: going almost seven years without improving one inch, just driven by my determination and the belief that I could do it.

Finally in June 1980 at the US Olympic trials I placed second and so earned a spot on the team and the title of US Olympian. Unfortunately President Carter had ordered a boycott of the Olympics to be held in Moscow, so for the third time politics prevented me from actually competing.

Although I never had the opportunity to compete in the Olympics, making the US team in 1980 really fulfilled my ambitions. The selection process is tough and there's a tremendous amount of pressure as you only get one chance every four years. As soon as it became obvious that I would finish in the top three at the Olympic trials, and therefore qualify for the team, I was overcome with so many emotions. Most of all was relief that after so many years of training, frustration, and sacrifice, I had qualified for the greatest Olympic team in the world, but there were also feelings of disappointment that all athletes on the team would miss out on the opportunity to achieve the ambition of competing at the Olympics.

I was fortunate to compete all over the world in a international competitions and while the Olympics are the most important to any amateur athlete, I don't consider my career a failure for not actually competing in them. Just making the US Olympic team is something I will always be proud of.

Bruce proves that adversity builds character. He trained all his life to become a champion javelin thrower. He qualified for three Olympic teams, but because of politics and boycotts he was not allowed to compete. Bruce is probably the only top ten Javelin thrower in the world to not compete in the Olympics. And rather than being bitter about his situation, he's grateful for the experience and proud of his accomplishments. That's character.

Tom Hoff
Volleyball - USA
Sydney 2000; Athens 2004; Beijing 2008

Tom Hoff has competed in three Summer Olympics for the US in Volleyball. He has a degree in Mechanical Engineering from Long Beach State University. He is also a partner account manager for Predixion Software in California.

Meet Hard Times with a Harder Will

I started playing volleyball when I was 15. Soon after I had visions of one day competing and trying to earn the right to win a Gold medal and be an Olympian for my country. It was a dream and vision that completely took control of my life. It drove the next 20 years of my life to try and accomplish. Almost all of my life choices were made to try to give me the best opportunity to actually realize my dream. I played the game of volleyball for over twenty plus years and it took me literately all over the planet chasing the goal that I set in my younger years.

Obviously on a journey of twenty years, every person will encounter a tremendous amount of hardships. Struggles are an inevitable part of accomplishing goals. Typically the more rewarding your dreams can be, the struggles that you face will seem insurmountable. But in the process of overcoming these issues that interrupt your path to your dream, you start to build your inner strength to a point where you will do not accept the act of failing. Every stumble becomes a learning experience, every unsuccessful moment becomes a chance in your journey to remind yourself that you need to constantly re-evaluate and re-tool your process of achieving your life long dreams.

After it was all said and done, the journey towards the team and myself earning a Gold medal and becoming an Olympic Champion gives me the self confidence that there is no goal that I cannot accomplish if myself and others dedicate every part of their body and mind to one single minded goal. This is an incredibly difficult task in itself but the rewards of success will last literately a lifetime. In the act of setting clear, well defined, ambitious goals, if you are willing to put the time, energy, and effort towards it, there is nothing that can stop you. There is no magic secret in achieving your dreams, just the attitude of putting the incredible amount of work and time that is necessary to attain them.

Tom dedicated twenty years of his life to the pursuit of his Olympic dream. He knew there would be struggles but he understood that as long as he didn't quit, the struggles would make him stronger. When you work long and hard for however long it takes and you start accomplishing big dreams you too will develop the self confidence that makes you realize that you really can accomplish anything you set your mind to.

Frankie Andreu
Cycling - USA
Seoul 1988; Atlanta 1996

Frankie Andreu competed in nine Tour de France races in his 12-year professional career. He competed in two Summer Olympics and he's a coach, a racing team director, a professional speaker and a cycling TV commentator.

Follow Your Passion

The obstacles I ran into when I tried to make the Olympics stemmed more from me not being a very good cyclist early on. When I first started racing, I didn't stand out. It took a long time for me to get to a level where I could race the races and not just ride the races. In my early races I would have trouble just staying with the other riders. As I got older I matured and got stronger and then I started to have ideas about making the Olympics. The key here was that I raced because it was fun; it was my passion regardless of if I did well or finished poorly. I bike raced and I loved it. I believe my love for cycling helped me continue and allowed me to make a living as a professional.

My first Olympic experience was in 1988 and then in 1996. Both were very different experiences. In 1988 I dreamed of making the Olympic team. It was a goal of mine and something I wanted very badly. In 1988 at the Seoul Olympics, I was younger than the more experienced riders that I raced against. I had trained extremely hard and was as prepared as I could be. I was very nervous during my first races and the riders I competed against were very fast and good. I knew I didn't have a chance to win, but I had to make sure to race well to represent the U.S. In the race things went well and I ended up in 8th place which I was pleased with. The entire trip was very overwhelming and a big eye opener.

In 1996, I was older and had the experience to have a chance to win. This time I knew what to expect and again I was physically prepared to race hard. The difference in 1996 was that there was a lot more pressure on me to do well. It was pressure I put on myself with expectations and outside pressure from the fans and public. Again, I had a good ride

197

and finished 4th. I was happy with this result.

To compete in the Olympics was an important goal in my life and in my cycling career. It set me up for a better future in my sport and gave me the confidence to know that I could compete on the world level as well as anyone else. During my career my goals changed as they did with the Olympics. At the start it's a learning curve and a bit of survival. Then it changed to trying to win the biggest races. Finally, it was staying on top of the sport for as long as possible. I get asked many times what some of my best memories are from my racing days and the Olympics are at the very top.

Frankie's love for cycling kept him in the game long enough to improve and to eventually become a champion. Dedicate your life to following a dream you are passionate about. If you do, you will make your life an adventure.

Michael Blatchford
Cycling - USA
Beijing 2008

Michael Blatchford grew up in Southern California where he was homeschooled through high school. He competed in cycling at the 2008 Beijing Olympics. Michael also regularly gives back to his local community, assisting with Boy Scout Bike Rodeo helmet fittings, working as an audio engineer for children's musical productions, and visiting with children's hospital patients. Michael lives in Colorado Springs.

Find a Higher Purpose

Many Olympians I know have thought about winning a gold medal since they were young. I was different. I just like to compete. I was always an active kid and played hard whatever sport I was in. I did gymnastics and played tennis before I found track cycling, and even then I only thought it was really cool simply to compete. I never imagined I would be an Olympian myself. I found pleasure in reaching all the little goals it takes along the way to become an Olympian. I started going a little faster in training, lifting more in the gym, and placing higher in races. When I was admitted into the residency program at the Olympic Training Center in Colorado Springs, making it to the Olympics became a goal.

The possibility of representing my country in the greatest of sporting events was very motivating, but I wouldn't call it a "dream." However, once I won the Olympic trials and knew there was a ticket to Beijing with my name on it, I think the goal became the dream and the dream a reality, all in a single moment.

I would have to say my struggles snuck up on me. Injuries are a part of life for athletes, but I also had several chronic health complications that make being competitive at this level a huge challenge. I questioned why I was putting myself through so much misery just for sport. "Even if I have success beyond everything I could hope for, what is the purpose? What if I were to achieve fame and fortune? Is there any lasting value in that?" I came to realize that the God-given gift I have as a cyclist is something I can only develop for a short time of my life. To paraphrase the Bible from 1 Corinthians – "Whatever I do, I should do for the glory of God." I may win a gold medal before I am finished, or I might not, but I can guarantee you that I will find fulfillment and satisfaction in doing my best for the One who gave me the ability in the first place.

The dream for me was fulfilled when I walked into the arena at the Opening Ceremonies. For the anniversary of the Beijing Games, I was asked to write an account of my experience. It can be summed up with this excerpt: "The American flag held high, and the anticipation as thick as ever, we began our entrance into the Bird's Nest and the beginning of the 2008 Olympic Games. No one will ever know who started the chant, but it instantly took over every American: 'U-S-A! U-S-A! U-S-A! U-S-A!'" The chant of 600 athletes, coaches and staff who had sacrificed years, even decades of their lives and their very bodies in the ultimate pursuit of physical ability and will, will resonate in my mind forever."

Michael had a higher purpose that helped him overcome the struggles he faced on the way to the Olympics. His faith in God and his desire to use his God-given gifts and talent for the glory of God was his driving force. What's your driving force? Having a higher purpose will help you perform better because it inspires you to give it your all. At the Salt Lake City Olympics, Dad met a Hungarian Bobsledder who was a cancer survivor. Her driving force to become an Olympian was to show other cancer survivors that cancer will knock you down but it does not have to knock you out. Find a higher purpose that will inspire you to perform at your best.

"The triumph can't be had without the struggle."

- Wilma Rudolph
1960 Track

Tim Seaman
Race Walker - USA
Sydney 2000; Athens 2004

Tim Seaman competed in race walking at the 2000 and 2004 Summer Olympics. He won the 5000 meter race walk at the USA Indoor Track and Field Championships 12 times. Tim has a Masters in International Relations from the University of San Diego. Today, Tim is currently the Cross Country, Women's Track and Field, and distance running coach, for Cuyamaca College in California.

The Dream is Worth the Pain

I had my first Olympic Dream in July 2000 when I won the USA Track and Field Olympic Trials 20km race walk competition. I won the race in a new meet record time. It was an amazing experience for me to come into the Olympic Trials Stadium in Sacramento with tons of people cheering for me, but most of all, it was great to have my parents and my sister there to cheer me on.

My biggest struggle happened about three years before the 2000 Olympic Trials. In August 1997, I started to have a pain in my lower abdominal area. I couldn't sit up in bed without being in pain, and I had to roll out of bed to get out of it. I was living at the Olympic Training Center, and I had rotating doctors that would come in every two weeks as volunteers. None of them could figure out what was wrong with me. Finally, with the help of Vinny Comiskey, the Head Trainer, I was able to figure out what the problem was and found out that I would need surgery to correct it.

The surgery was extremely painful. I was unable to sit up straight for four weeks, and it took seven weeks before I was able to exercise for the first time. I ran just four minutes that first day. Every day was a struggle. People around me were telling me that I was done, that I would never race walk again, but I didn't want to listen to them. I had to work so hard to come back from that surgery, but every day I kept thinking about my dream of representing the United States at the world's biggest sporting event. Every day there was just one focus, just one goal. I put my body through so much pain, but in the end, nothing could compare to walking in to the Olympic Stadium behind the American Flag with over 100,000 people watching the Opening Ceremonies of the

2000 Olympic Games in Sydney, Australia.

It is difficult to describe the feeling of walking behind the American Flag as I entered the Olympic Stadium, knowing that I finally accomplished my lifelong dream of representing my family at the Olympic Games. When I crossed the finish line of the Olympic Trials, the smile on my parents' faces and also that of my sister, Jaime, was like being able to buy your parents everything they ever wanted all in an instant. It was truly amazing.

Tim has to come back from a very painful surgery to get to compete in the Olympics. Every step of his comeback he faced extreme pain. His desire to become an Olympian drove him to continue training through the pain even when everyone told him he was through. General Patton said that the body is weaker than the mind. Your body will tell you to quit as soon as it feels uncomfortable, but you can train your mind to be stronger than your body. Champions are willing to work through the pain. If you are willing to work harder than your competition, you can become a champion and realize your dreams just like Tim Seaman did.

Kara Salmela
Biathlon - USA
Nagano 1998; Salt Lake City 2002

Kara Salmela competed in the biathlon at the 1998 Nagano and the 2002 Salt Lake City Winter Olympics. She also earned a degree in Exercise Science from the University of Minnesota-Duluth. Today Kara is a business manager for the Med Search Network.

Never Ever Quit

The Olympic creed was the motto that kept me going throughout my struggle to become an Olympic Biathlete. It reads: "The most important thing in the Olympic Games is not to win but to take part, just as the most important thing in life is not the triumph but the struggle. The essential thing is not to have conquered but to have fought well."

It is easy to lose sight on what is really important when you are pursuing a goal like making an Olympic Team. The Olympic creed points out that like sports, life is not about winning but the struggle to reach your goals. I first wanted to become an Olympian when I was invited to a training camp in Lake Placid, New York in 1992. I was recruited by the US Biathlon Association from college skiing. After meeting the National Biathlon team, staying in the training center, and falling in love with the sport, I was hooked and wanted to make the 1998 team. I started training full-time to reach my goal the day after I left the camp.

It was not easy, and I struggled to learn to shoot and ski at a high level for many years. There were three very important things I needed to overcome before I could make the Olympic team in 1998. The first struggle was my health. I was fighting chronic sinus infections that left me unable to train for weeks and follow a normal training plan. In 1995 a doctor explained that I would have to eliminate the foods that I was allergic to from my diet and go on a cleansing diet to rebuild my immunity. It took me almost two years to feel normal again and train at a high level. Then the next problem I encountered was severe shin splints that left me unable to run and shoot during the summer training months. Unfortunately, running and shooting were two of the most important workouts we needed to do. Until there was snow to ski on, I was unable to run for training so I had to focus on roller skiing, staying mentally strong and gaining fitness through other training methods. Finally, the last fight I had to battle was my shooting scores. I had to bring my overall shooting percentage up in order to be good enough to make the team. I started doing a lot of mental training, and using a relaxation tape that helped me calm down for shooting. With this I could do more shooting drills than I had ever done before.

All of my training and attention to detail paid off the day of our first Olympic trial race. I hit 18 out of 20 targets and out-skied the field by over 90 seconds, putting me in first place and way ahead in the overall points. All I had to do was have two more good races, and I would make the team. Consequently, I made the team. My preparation and focus for that first race sealed my spot on the 1998 Olympic Team and made my Olympic dream come true.

Realizing this dream was the biggest accomplishment of my life. It was an unbelievable feeling walking into opening ceremonies in Japan and sharing this moment with the rest of the world. It made me reflect on everyone who helped me reach my dream and encouraged me along the way. It also solidified the Olympic motto, as I felt that although participating in the Olympics was the highlight, it was really the day to day struggle and overcoming those obstacles that made the experience fantastic.

Most people quit on their dream even before they get started. They focus on why they can't do something instead of figuring a way to overcome their challenges. Kara's sinus infections and shin splints made it hard for her to train in the summer months. And her shooting was sub par. Instead of quitting, Kara tackled her challenges head-on. Over two years she strengthened her immunity by changing her diet, she roller bladed in the summer instead of running, and she learned how to strengthen her mind so that she could improve her shooting. Kara's driving force was competing in the Olympics. It was not about winning. It was about competing. The same was true for Dad. His driving force was not to win a medal. It was simply to get to compete in the Olympics and to be a part of that special group of people who are willing to sacrifice everything for a dream.

Donald Suxho
Volleyball - USA
Athens 2004

Donald Suxho was born in Albania. He's a professional volleyball player who competed for the US Team at the 2004 Athens Olympics and the 2012 London Olympics. Suxho and his family came to the U.S. in 1996 and lived in Massachusetts while searching for a college. He eventually chose to play for the University of Southern California, where he earned a degree in Communications.

Focus on what You Can Control

I never dreamed of going to the Olympics, simply because I could not. I grew up in Albania under a communist regime, and we were told how to think, act, what to study, and where to work. There was no freedom of speech or thought. I came to USA when I was 18 and was lucky enough to go to USC and play volleyball there for four years. As my career grew, I was invited to USA National Team for a tryout in 2000. From that moment I began dreaming about being on the team. One year before the Olympics, in 2003, I started to dream and hope I could be on the team, and it became true in 2004 in Athens.

In volleyball, it takes four years to prepare, train, and qualify. Unfortunately, I was cut from the team after my 1st year, and it was my fault. I selfishly wanted to play every game, so I didn't pay attention to teamwork and improving myself. After the 2nd year I was given a second chance and really focused on improving every day and on being the best teammate on and off the court. I understood that if I sacrificed more of my own effort and playing time to my team, the result would be bigger than what I thought before. I learned how to accept criticism, accept fear, and accept days when I played badly. I would wake up the next morning and really focus on becoming a better player than the day before. I learned how to focus on things that I could control, such as my position, my playing, my attitude, my effort, and leave the rest to the coach, trusting my team, and our system.

At the Olympics I cried, I jumped, I ran, and I was like a child. I still don't believe it. It's the best feeling in the world, because I worked so hard for four years. I sacrificed, overcame injuries, changed my way of thinking, changed

213

the way I lived my life on and off the court, became more responsible and invested all my energy and effort to reach the big goal and dream, the Olympics. To say that hard work pays off, is 100% true.

Donald was cut from his volleyball team for being a selfish player. Then he made a decision to become a selfless team player. To focus on what he could focus on and not worry about the rest. He made it is mission to improve every day. Donald transformed himself. And you can too. You can make your dream come true because you have the ability to change. You can get better. Every day in every way you can get better and better. Stronger and stronger. Wiser and wiser. And before long you will have transformed yourself into the kind of person who can reach your dream.

Emily Cook
Freestyle Skiing - USA
Torino 2006; Vancouver 2010

Emily Cook is an American freestyle skier. She competed in the 2006 Torino Olympics and in the 2010 Vancouver Olympics. She's a five time US National Champion. Emily has a degree in Mass Communications from the University of Utah. Today she is a columnist for Ski Racing Magazine.

Bounce Back Quickly

I was 13 years old when I first decided that I wanted to be an Olympian. I had recently discovered the sport of freestyle aerial skiing, which was the perfect combination of my two favorite sports: gymnastics and skiing. I completely loved the feeling of flipping on skis. In the summer of 1992, a coach asked me what my goals were, and I had no idea. I sat with my Dad and thought about what I wanted. I realized that in ten years, in 2002, would be the perfect time to compete in my first Olympics. So, I wrote it down and I trained diligently and intently for the next ten years.

Ten years later on New Year's Eve of 2002, I finally had the chance to realize that dream. The U.S. Ski Team held an Olympic Trial in Utah. The venue was at the very site that the 2002 Salt Lake City Olympic Games would be held. In my hometown of Park City and at my favorite ski resort, Deer Valley where the year before I had been on my first World Cup podium.

The Olympic stands were already in place and the venue was filled with 15,000 Olympic enthusiasts, it was amazing. That night I won the Olympic Trial and secured myself a spot on the 2002 United States Winter Olympic Team. I was overwhelmed with emotion and happiness. My biggest dream had just come true and I was so excited to represent my country six weeks later! Sadly, that was not to happen. Three weeks later, while training for a World Cup in Lake Placid, New York a windy day caused me to misjudge my speed coming into a jump. I landed on the flat part of the hill, shattering both of my feet. Instead of competing in my first Olympic Games, I would watch from the stands in a wheelchair.

Watching the opening ceremony of the Salt Lake City Winter Olympics from a wheelchair with tears on my cheeks made me realize that I would do absolutely everything I could to get to the next Olympics in Torino. After years of rehabilitation I was able to compete again, and at the next Olympic Trial I won with an overwhelming lead over my fellow competitors, guaranteeing myself a spot on the US Olympic Team for the 2006 Winter Olympic Games in Torino. Walking into the opening ceremony of the 2006 Winter Olympic Games in Torino with the teammates who had supported me throughout my injury and rehabilitation was the most wonderful day of my life. Having overcome so much to be there made it even more special and to this day it is one of my most favorite memories.

Imagine training for ten years, qualifying in first place, having the opportunity to compete in the Winter Olympics in your hometown, and breaking both feet only three weeks before the Opening Ceremonies. It happened to Emily. Like a true winner, she took strength and conviction from her struggle and came back stronger than ever. When life knocks you down, determine to get back up and to fight harder than ever before.

Margaret Hoelzer
USA - Swimming
Athens 2004; Beijing 2008

Margaret Hoelzer swam for the US. She's an Olympic medalist, and former world record-holder. Holzer competed in the 2004 Olympic Games in Athens, Greece, and the 2008 Olympic Games in Beijing, China. Margaret is a professional speaker and the National Spokesperson for the National Children's Advocacy Center.

220

Give Yourself Time to Improve

I first wanted to go to the Olympics after seeing it on TV at the age of 9. At that point I didn't really know what the Olympics were, or what it took to get there. I began swimming at age five in summer league and then started swimming year round when I was 8. As I got older, I made other goals that were more realistic for the time, but the Olympics were always a long term goal that I had.

I was very good at an early age. Being very tall was my main struggle, as because of this I grew early which made me hit plateaus later on in my swimming career. I had a four year plateau from age 14-18. During this plateau I literally didn't get any faster for four years, not even a little bit. Also because of this I was recruited to swim in college based on times I had done as a 14-year-old. These were good times for 14, but very average for 18. Fortunately, there was a coach who had seen me swim when I was younger and believe that there was still something in me that hadn't been accomplished yet.

I went on to swim in college at Auburn University where I had success for a few years, including making my first Olympic team in 2004. However, I hit a second plateau that lasted for three and a half years, from 2003 to 2007. While I made the Olympic team in 2004, I didn't swim very well there or at any other international competition for the next few years. It wasn't until the World Championships in 2007 that I broke off of this plateau and went on to win Worlds which then carried into a very successful 2008 Olympic trials and games for me.

Making your dreams come true has many meanings. I had the swims of a lifetime in the 2008 Olympics, and I certainly feel that I accomplished my goals there. However, I'm very proud of the fact that I had to overcome a lot to get to those goals. I've been asked if I wanted to quit and the answer is yes, I wanted to quit many times, but I didn't. I stuck to what I believed in and made my dreams a reality. That is an accomplishment that I'm very proud of.

If you work hard and you believe in something you can always achieve it. To be honest with yourself is very important, because a lot of people don't realize when they truly are or are not trying their best. Another thing I learned was that doing your best is about your best on any given day. My times at the Olympic Games in 2008 were slightly slower than they were at trials, but I am still very proud of those swims because they were the best that I could have done on that day. Another really important thing to me is having fun. I had an amazing time in Beijing and that showed in my performance.

Margaret went through two long periods where her times did not improve. But she continued training with the hope that she would get stronger and eventually improve. Most people don't understand how frustrating a plateau can be for an athlete. It's a huge test for your belief. Imagine going on a diet in order to lose 15 pounds. You lose 10 pounds in the first 6 weeks but you just can't seem to lose the last five pounds. What do you do? Do you give up, go on a binge and regain all the weight? Or do you stick with your diet and try different exercise programs hoping that you'll eventually lose the weight? If you are not getting the results you want, don't quit. Try different approaches and eventually you'll get through your plateau.

Ruben Gonzalez
Luge - Argentina
Calgary 1988; Albertville 1992;
Salt Lake City 2002; Vancouver 2010

Ruben Gonzalez is my dad. He competed for Argentina in the luge. Dad's the only person to ever compete in four Winter Olympics each in a different decade. He was 47 years old when he competed in the 2010 Vancouver Winter Olympics. Dad graduated from Houston Baptist University with degrees in Biology and Chemistry. He is a best selling author and an award winning professional speaker.

Have the Courage to Succeed

When I was 10 years old, I was watching the 1972 Sapporo Winter Olympics on TV and I knew right away that I wanted to be an Olympian. I was drawn to the Olympic athletes. What drew me to them wasn't their athleticism, it was their spirit. The Olympians were a group of people that were willing to fight for their dream for many years with no guarantees of success. From that day on I read everything I could about the Olympics. I could tell you everything about the Olympics but I was afraid of taking action because I was never a great athlete. In fact, in PE at school, I was always the last kid they picked to play ports.

Several years went by. I remember being glued to the TV whenever the Olympics were on. In 1980, when the US Miracle Hockey Team beat the Russians at the Lake Placid Olympics, my belief started growing. I was re-inspired but my fear still kept me from taking action. Finally, in 1984 I saw Scott Hamilton win the Gold Medal in figure skating. When I saw Scott win, I said to myself, "If that little guy can do it, so can I. I'll be in the next Olympics. It's a done deal. I just have to find a sport." Watching Scott Hamilton's performance lit a fire in me. I was finally ready to take action. I was 21 years old.

I had no time to lose. The next Olympics were only four years away and I had to find a sport. I went to the library to do some research. When I looked at a list of the Summer Olympic Sports I said to myself, "You have to be a super athlete to do any of these things. There's no way." Then I took a list of the Winter Olympic sports. I realized I needed to find a sport that fit my strengths. My strength wasn't athleticism. My strength was perseverance. In fact my nickname in High

225

School was "Bulldog." So I thought, "I have to find a sport that's so tough, a sport with so many broken bones in it, that there will be a lot of quitters. Only I won't quit. I'll make it to the top through the attrition rate."

I had it down to three sports. Ski jump, bobsled, and luge. I lived in Houston, Texas. Hot, humid, sticky Houston. I'd never skied before so forget ski jump. That would have been suicide. And bobsled? Where was I going to find three other people in Houston that would want to do the bobsled? That left the luge. I'd never even seen the luge on TV before. If I had, I doubt if I had done it. It's crazy. All I had was a picture of a guy on a luge. I said to myself, "That's the sport for me." That's how I picked my sport.

I didn't even know where the luge track was. So I wrote Sports Illustrated and asked them, "Where do you go to learn how to do the luge?" They wrote back saying the track was in Lake Placid. I called the Luge Association in Lake Placid and got myself into a beginners program. Just a couple of months after watching Scott Hamilton win the Gold in the Sarajevo Olympics I was in Lake Placid learning how to luge.

They put me in a class with fifteen other brand new sliders. It was brutal. The toughest thing I've ever done. Every day a couple of less people would show up for practice. By the end of the first season I was the only one left from that group. The first two years I was crashing four out of five times. But I kept at it. After a while I was crashing only one out of five times. Then one out of ten. By the end of the second year I was crashing only one out of a hundred. I finally figured out how to drive that crazy sled.

Over the first few years I broke my foot twice, my knee, my elbow, my hand, my thumb, and a couple of ribs. My attitude was that a broken bone was just a temporary inconvenience, because bones heal. On the third season I started competing internationally to try to qualify for the

1988 Calgary Olympics. On the fourth year I made it. I got to compete in four Olympics by the skin on my teeth. Four Olympics each in a different decade. As I jokingly tell my audiences, "It doesn't mean I'm good. It just means I'm old!"

Marching in the Opening Ceremonies is the highlight of the Olympics. You don't march into the stadium. You float in. For two weeks you walk around with a silly smile on your face. It's Heaven. It really is. Competing in the Olympics was worth every sacrifice. It was worth getting hurt. It was worth driving a beat up old car. It was worth maxing out my credit cards and getting into a huge debt. It was worth the years of hard training and the bitter cold.

I'm a better person for having put myself through the struggle. I'm stronger, more confident, and I've learned things about myself that will help me for the rest of my life.

What were the chances that someone like me would make it to the Olympics? One in a million? One in ten million? I probably had a better chance to win the lottery!

I was just an ordinary kid with an extraordinary dream. I wasn't a big shot. I was a little shot that kept on shooting. Just like that young, scrappy U.S. Hockey Team that beat the mighty Russians. Just like Scott Hamilton. That's all they did. They believed in themselves and they just kept on shooting.

And that's something you can do too. If you start believing in yourself, you give it all you've got, and you refuse to quit, it will be just a matter of time before you make your dream come true, too; and just a matter of time before you start creating a better life.

Success is a choice. It's your choice. Make a decision that you will face your fears and do whatever it takes to get started. Make the decision to get off the stands and into the arena. Make the decision to stop existing and to start living.

Because if this little shot did what he did, then you can do anything.

What's your Olympics? What's your dream? If you will dedicate your life to the pursuit of your dream like my dad and all these other Olympians did, you will be making your life a masterpiece. You will live a rich life and you too will be an inspiration to everyone around you.

"Each of us has a fire in our hearts for something. It's our goal in life to find it and keep it lit."

- Mary Lou Retton
1984 Gymnastics

Afterword

After reading these stories, I hope you realize that there is nothing special about any of these Olympians. They were just ordinary people who had a burning desire and were willing to do whatever it took, for as long as it took, to make it happen.

They just consistently and persistently followed timeless success principles. They believed in their dream, they planned ahead, they committed to their dream, they took massive action, and they had the character to endure when the going got tough.

Do yourself a favor: don't just read these principles. Apply them. Knowledge is not power. Applied knowledge is power.

This book is proof that these principles will work for anyone. If you start believing in yourself, you give it all you've got, and you refuse to quit, it will be just a matter of time before you make your dream come true, too; and just a matter of time before you start creating a better life.

Success is a choice. It's your choice. Make a decision that you will face your fears and do whatever it takes to get started. Make the decision to get off the stands and into the arena. Make the decision to stop existing and to start living. And you too will reach your own personal Olympics. You will create a magnificent life and you will become an inspiration to everyone around you.

Fight for your Dream!

About the Authors

Gabriela Gonzalez, a 14 years old native Texan, now residing in Colorado Springs, Colorado, has been homeschooled all her life. She loves playing the piano and singing Christian and Broadway songs. Gabriela also competes in Judo and trains at the Olympic Training Center. When she is not creating stories, Gabriela enjoys hiking in the Rocky Mountains, snowboarding,

acting, and spending time with friends.

Gabriela is blessed with a love for writing. She's the author of *"My Magic Snowshoes."*

Ruben Gonzalez wasn't a gifted athlete. He didn't take up the sport of luge until he was 21. Against all odds, four years, and a few broken bones later, he was competing in the Calgary Winter Olympics. At the age of 47 he was racing against 20-year-olds in the Vancouver Olympics.

As a four-time Olympian, peak-performance expert and business author Ruben Gonzalez knows how to achieve success.

As a master storyteller and keynote speaker, Ruben uses his Olympic experiences to inspire audiences to think differently, live life with passion and have the courage to take the necessary steps toward their goals – to push beyond self-imposed limitations and to produce better results.

Ruben's appeared nationally on ABC, CBS, NBC and FOX. He's been featured in Time Magazine, BusinessWeek, The New York Times as well as publications in all over the world. His articles on peak-performance are read in every continent.

His clients include, Xerox, Oracle, Coca-Cola, Microsoft, Oracle, Shell Oil, United Airlines, Farmers Insurance, Johnson & Johnson, Ortho McNeal, Blue Cross Blue Shield, Wells Fargo, RE/MAX, New York Life, The U.S. Treasury Department and many more.

Ruben lives in Colorado with his wife Cheryl and their children Gabriela and Gracen. He enjoys the challenge of climbing Colorado's fourteen-thousand-foot peaks, snowboarding, and sailing.

Join the Thousands of high achievers who have learned how to become unstoppable on the way to success.

Sign up for Ruben's Monthly Success Tips

To subscribe visit:

www.FourWinterGames.com

Book Ruben for Your Next Event

To have Ruben speak to your organization or to order any of his other personal and professional development products call:

832-689-8282

www.FourWinterGames.com